EVOLUTION
Change Over Time

Anthea Maton
Former NSTA National Coordinator
Project Scope, Sequence, Coordination
Washington, DC

Jean Hopkins
Science Instructor and Department Chairperson
John H. Wood Middle School
San Antonio, Texas

Susan Johnson
Professor of Biology
Ball State University
Muncie, Indiana

David LaHart
Senior Instructor
Florida Solar Energy Center
Cape Canaveral, Florida

Maryanna Quon Warner
Science Instructor
Del Dios Middle School
Escondido, California

Jill D. Wright
Professor of Science Education
Director of International Field Programs
University of Pittsburgh
Pittsburgh, Pennsylvania

PRENTICE HALL
Upper Saddle River, New Jersey
Needham, Massachusetts

Prentice Hall Science

Evolution: Change Over Time

Student Text	**Study Guide**
Annotated Teacher's Edition	**Integrated Science Activity Book**
Teacher's Resource Package	**Integrated Science Activity Book II**
Laboratory Manual	**Computer Test Bank**
Activity Book	**Transparency Binder**
Test Book	**Teacher's Desk Reference**
Review and Reinforcement	**Product Testing Activities**
Guide	**Prentice Hall Science Integrated Media**

The illustration on the cover, rendered by Keith Kasnot, shows a modern iguana with the bones of an ancient dinosaur in the background.

Credits begin on page 117.

THIRD EDITION

ISBN 0-13-423450-2

6 7 8 9 10   00 99 98

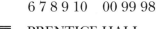

PRENTICE HALL
Simon & Schuster Education Group
A Viacom Company

STAFF CREDITS

Editorial:	Lorraine Smith-Phelan, Maureen Grassi, Christine Caputo, Joseph Berman, Rekha Sheorey, Matthew Hart, Kathleen Ventura
Technology Development:	Ted Tolles
Design:	AnnMarie Roselli, Laura Bird, Gerry Schrenk, Monduane Harris
Production:	Christina Burghard, Gertrude Szyferblatt, Elizabeth Torjussen, Gregory Myers, Cleasta Wilburn
Media Resources:	Libby Forsyth, Emily Rose, Martha Conway, Vickie Menanteaux, Suzi Myers
Marketing:	Andrew Socha, Jane Walker Neff, Victoria Willows
Pre-Press Production:	Kathryn Dix, Carol Barbara, Marie McNamara
Manufacturing:	Loretta Moe, Matt McCabe
National Science Consultants:	Kathy French, Jeannie Dennard, Patricia M. Cominsky, Charles Balko, Brenda Underwood

Contributing Writers

Linda Densman
Science Instructor
Hurst, TX

Linda Grant
Former Science Instructor
Weatherford, TX

Heather Hirschfeld
Science Writer
Durham, NC

Marcia Mungenast
Science Writer
Upper Montclair, NJ

Michael Ross
Science Writer
New York City, NY

Content Reviewers

Dan Anthony
Science Mentor
Rialto, CA

John Barrow
Science Instructor
Pomona, CA

Leslie Bettencourt
Science Instructor
Harrisville, RI

Stuart Birnbaum
Geologist
Helotes, TX

Carol Bishop
Science Instructor
Palm Desert, CA

Dan Bohan
Science Instructor
Palm Desert, CA

Steve M. Carlson
Science Instructor
Milwaukie, OR

Larry Flammer
Science Instructor
San Jose, CA

Steve Ferguson
Science Instructor
Lee's Summit, MO

Robin Lee Harris Freedman
Science Instructor
Fort Bragg, CA

Edith H. Gladden
Former Science Instructor
Philadelphia, PA

Vernita Marie Graves
Science Instructor
Tenafly, NJ

Jack Grube
Science Instructor
San Jose, CA

Emiel Hamberlin
Science Instructor
Chicago, IL

Dwight Kertzman
Science Instructor
Tulsa, OK

Judy Kirschbaum
Science/Computer Instructor
Tenafly, NJ

John F. Koser
Physics/Astronomy Instructor
Plymouth, MN

Kenneth L. Krause
Science Instructor
Milwaukie, OR

Ernest W. Kuehl, Jr.
Science Instructor
Bayside, NY

Mary Grace Lopez
Science Instructor
Corpus Christi, TX

Philip M. Lurie
Former Research Chemist
Paramus, NJ

Warren Maggard
Science Instructor
PeWee Valley, KY

Della M. McCaughan
Science Instructor
Biloxi, MS

Stanley J. Mulak
Former Science Instructor
Jensen Beach, FL

Richard Myers
Science Instructor
Portland, OR

Carol Nathanson
Science Mentor
Riverside, CA

Sylvia Neivert
Former Science Instructor
San Diego, CA

Jarvis VNC Pahl
Science Instructor
Rialto, CA

Kevin Reel
Science Department Chairperson
Ojai, CA

Arlene Sackman
Science Instructor
Tulare, CA

Christine Schumacher
Science Instructor
Pikesville, MD

Suzanne Steinke
Science Instructor
Towson, MD

Len Svinth
Science Instructor/ Chairperson
Petaluma, CA

Elaine M. Tadros
Science Instructor
Palm Desert, CA

Susan J. Thomas
Science Instructor
Haverhill, MA

Joyce K. Walsh
Science Instructor
Midlothian, VA

Charlene West, PhD
Director of Curriculum
Rialto, CA

John Westwater
Science Instructor
Medford, MA

Glenna Wilkoff
Science Instructor
Chesterfield, OH

Edee Norman Wiziecki
Science Instructor
Urbana, IL

Teacher Advisory Panel

Beverly Brown
Science Instructor
Livonia, MI

James Burg
Science Instructor
Cincinnati, OH

Karen M. Cannon
Science Instructor
San Diego, CA

John Eby
Science Instructor
Richmond, CA

Elsie M. Jones
Science Instructor
Marietta, GA

Michael Pierre McKereghan
Science Instructor
Denver, CO

Donald D. Pace, Sr.
Science Instructor
Reisterstown, MD

Carlos Francisco Sainz
Science Instructor
National City, CA

William Reed
Science Instructor
Indianapolis, IN

Multicultural Consultant

Steven J. Rakow
Associate Professor
University of Houston— Clear Lake
Houston, TX

English as a Second Language (ESL) Consultants

Jaime Morales
Bilingual Coordinator
Huntington Park, CA

Pat Hollis Smith
Former ESL Instructor
Beaumont, TX

Reading Consultant

Larry Swinburne
Director
Swinburne Readability Laboratory

CONTENTS

EVOLUTION: CHANGE OVER TIME

Activity Bank/Reference Section

Features

CONCEPT MAPPING

Throughout your study of science, you will learn a variety of terms, facts, figures, and concepts. Each new topic you encounter will provide its own collection of words and ideas—which, at times, you may think seem endless. But each of the ideas within a particular topic is related in some way to the others. No concept in science is isolated. Thus it will help you to understand the topic if you see the whole picture; that is, the interconnectedness of all the individual terms and ideas. This is a much more effective and satisfying way of learning than memorizing separate facts.

Actually, this should be a rather familiar process for you. Although you may not think about it in this way, you analyze many of the elements in your daily life by looking for relationships or connections. For example, when you look at a collection of flowers, you may divide them into groups: roses, carnations, and daisies. You may then associate colors with these flowers: red, pink, and white. The general topic is flowers. The subtopic is types of flowers. And the colors are specific terms that describe flowers. A topic makes more sense and is more easily understood if you understand how it is broken down into individual ideas and how these ideas are related to one another and to the entire topic.

It is often helpful to organize information visually so that you can see how it all fits together. One technique for describing related ideas is called a **concept map**. In a concept map, an idea is represented by a word or phrase enclosed in a box. There are several ideas in any concept map. A connection between two ideas is made with a line. A word or two that describes the connection is written on or near the line. The general topic is located at the top of the map. That topic is then broken down into subtopics, or more specific ideas, by branching lines. The most specific topics are located at the bottom of the map.

To construct a concept map, first identify the important ideas or key terms in the chapter or section. Do not try to include too much information. Use your judgment as to what is really important. Write the general topic at the top of your map. Let's use an example to help illustrate this process. Suppose you decide that the key terms in a section you are reading are School, Living Things, Language Arts, Subtraction, Grammar, Mathematics, Experiments, Papers, Science, Addition, Novels. The general topic is School. Write and enclose this word in a box at the top of your map.

SCHOOL

Now choose the subtopics—Language Arts, Science, Mathematics. Figure out how they are related to the topic. Add these words to your map. Continue this procedure until you have included all the important ideas and terms. Then use lines to make the appropriate connections between ideas and terms. Don't forget to write a word or two on or near the connecting line to describe the nature of the connection.

Do not be concerned if you have to redraw your map (perhaps several times!) before you show all the important connections clearly. If, for example, you write papers for Science as well as for Language Arts, you may want to place these two subjects next to each other so that the lines do not overlap.

One more thing you should know about concept mapping: Concepts can be correctly mapped in many different ways. In fact, it is unlikely that any two people will draw identical concept maps for a complex topic. Thus there is no one correct concept map for any topic! Even

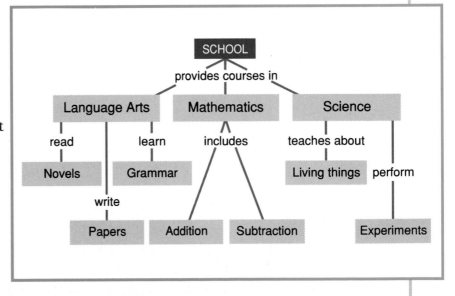

though your concept map may not match those of your classmates, it will be correct as long as it shows the most important concepts and the clear relationships among them. Your concept map will also be correct if it has meaning to you and if it helps you understand the material you are reading. A concept map should be so clear that if some of the terms are erased, the missing terms could easily be filled in by following the logic of the concept map.

EVOLUTION

Change Over Time

A gentle breeze sent ripples across the shimmering surface of the shallow pond. The ground shook slightly as a giant ground sloth walked clumsily out of the nearby woods. Dipping its head toward the water, the sloth drank deeply. Suddenly, the sloth raised its head and stood very still, trying to detect a whisper of danger from the trees.

Hearing nothing, the sloth bent its head toward the water again. At that moment, a saber-toothed cat leaped from the woods. With

▼ *Although neither the saber-toothed cat nor the ground sloth will survive its sticky encounter with the La Brea tar pits, its remains may become fossils found by scientists thousands of years in the future.*

claws bared and teeth flashing, the cat flew through the air toward its startled prey. With the giant cat on its back, the sloth plunged into the pond. Its feet splashed through the water but did not find solid ground. Instead, a sticky, gooey tar trapped the animal, pulling it further and further down into the pond.

In a matter of minutes, both animals were stuck in the tar. They remained there for thousands of years. In the early 1900s, scientists discovered their remains and pieced together a picture of the area in which the sloth and the cat had made their home. Today, this place is known as the La Brea tar pits in Los Angeles, California.

The types of fossils that were found in the La Brea pits are not the only kinds of fossils that have been found. As you read this book, you will discover some other types of evidence that help scientists gain an understanding of the Earth's past.

▲ *A model of an elephantlike creature trapped in tar can be seen at the La Brea tar pits in Los Angeles, California.*

Discovery *Activity*

Looking Into the Earth's Past

Take a walk through a nearby park or through your neighborhood and look for fossils embedded in the surfaces of sidewalks, building walls, rocks, and roads.

■ What do the fossils look like?

■ What do the fossils tell you about the kinds of living things that formed them?

■ How do you think the fossils formed?

Earth's History in Fossils

Guide for Reading

After you read the following sections, you will be able to

1–1 Fossils—Clues to the Past

■ Describe how scientists use fossils as clues to events in Earth's past.

1–2 A History in Rocks and Fossils

■ Define the law of superposition and describe how it is used to find the relative age of rocks and fossils.

■ Describe how the half-life of radioactive elements is used to find the absolute age of rocks and fossils.

1–3 A Trip Through Geologic Time

■ Describe the major life forms and geologic events that occurred in each geologic era.

A cloud of volcanic ash rises toward the sky above a strange landscape. Beneath the cloud, firs, pines, and tall palmlike trees sway in a warm, gentle breeze. Furry mammals, most no larger than a rat, scurry about on the forest floor. One day, descendants of these mammals will become the dominant animals on Earth. But that day is a long way off: The time is 140 million years ago, and the world belongs to the dinosaurs.

The world is changing, however. A great mountain chain is rising—a mountain chain that will eventually stretch from Alaska to Central America. Soon the landscape will be quite different. The Age of Dinosaurs will come to an end. All that will be left of these magnificent reptiles will be their bones.

One day in the distant future, a shepherd will build a cabin of dinosaur bones—the only such building in the world. Quite naturally, the place will be called Bone Cabin Quarry. And the vast area around it will be known as Wyoming!

In this chapter, you will learn about the Earth's past. You will also take a trip through time and discover many of the changes that have taken place in the Earth's 4.6-billion-year existence.

Journal *Activity*

You and Your World Although people and dinosaurs often do battle in Hollywood movies, all the dinosaurs were actually gone long before people evolved on Earth. But for now, imagine that you are alive during the Age of Dinosaurs. In your journal, write a brief story about a day in your life.

Slashing with their terrible sickle-shaped claws, a pack of fierce meat-eating dinosaurs attack an Iguanodon *in this scene from 140 million years ago.*

1–1 Fossils—Clues to the Past

The shepherd you have just read about used dinosaur bones to build Bone Cabin. Scientists use dinosaur bones, too, but for a different purpose. Dinosaur bones provide clues that help scientists build a different kind of structure—the structure of Earth's past. How exactly do they do this?

If you see a fish, you can conclude that somewhere on Earth there must be water, for that is where fishes live. If you see a polar bear, you can conclude that somewhere on Earth there is ice and cold temperatures—the environment in which polar bears live. In much the same way, scientists who study prehistoric forms of life use **fossils** to form a picture of Earth's past.

A fossil is the remains or evidence of a living thing. A fossil can be the bone of an organism or the print of a shell in a rock. A fossil can even be a burrow or tunnel left by an ancient worm. The most common fossils are bones, shells, pollen grains, and seeds.

Most fossils are not complete organisms. Fossils are generally incomplete because only the hard parts of dead plants or animals become fossils. The soft tissues either decay or are eaten before fossils can form. Decay is the breakdown of dead organisms into the substances from which they were made.

Figure 1–1 *Scientists carefully reassemble fossil bones to better understand the living things that existed long ago. What are fossils?*

Most ancient forms of life have left behind few, if any, fossils as evidence that they once lived on Earth. In fact, the chances of any plant or animal leaving a fossil are slight at best. For most fossils to form, the remains of organisms usually have to be buried in **sediments** soon after the organisms die. Sediments are small pieces of rocks, shells, and other materials that were broken down over time. Quick burial in sediments prevents the dead organisms from being eaten by animals. It also slows down or stops the decay process.

Plants and animals that lived in or near water were preserved more often than other organisms were. Sediments in the form of mud and sand could easily bury plants and animals that died in the water or along the sides of a body of water. When the sediments slowly hardened and changed to sedimentary rocks, the organisms were trapped in the rocks. Sedimentary rocks are formed from layers of sediments. Most fossils are found in sedimentary rocks.

Rocks known as igneous rocks are formed by the cooling and hardening of hot molten rock, or magma. Most magma is found deep within the Earth, where no living things exist. Sometimes the magma flows onto the Earth's surface as hot, fiery lava. Can you explain why fossils are almost never found in igneous rocks?

A third type of rock is called metamorphic rock. Metamorphic rocks are formed when sedimentary or igneous rocks are changed by heat, pressure, and chemical reactions. If there are fossils in a rock that undergoes such changes, the fossils are usually destroyed or damaged. So fossils are rarely found in metamorphic rocks as well.

There are many different kinds of fossils. Each kind is identified according to the process by which it was formed.

Petrification

When the dinosaurs died, the soft parts of their bodies quickly decayed. Only the hard parts—the bones—were left. Many of these bones were buried under layers of sediments of mud and wet sand. As water seeped through the layers of sediments, it dissolved minerals in the mud and sand. The water and

Figure 1–2 *These coiled shells once housed octopuslike animals that lived millions of years ago. How did the shells end up trapped in solid rock?*

ACTIVITY

Animal Footprints

1. Spread some mud in a low, flat-bottomed pan. Make sure the mud is not too wet and runny. Smooth the surface of the mud.

2. Have your pet or a neighbor's pet walk across the mud. Let the mud dry so that it hardens and the footprints are permanent.

3. Bring the footprints to science class. Exchange your set of footprints for the set of another student.

Examine the footprints and predict what type of animal made them. Explain how you arrived at your answer.

How is this activity similar to the way scientists determine what organism left the fossils that have been found?

Figure 1–3 *The Petrified Forest in Arizona has stone copies of trees that once grew there. The stone trees are the result of a process called petrification. How does petrification occur?*

minerals flowed through pores, or tiny holes, in the buried bones. When the water evaporated, the minerals were left behind in the bones, turning the bones to stone. This process is called **petrification,** which means turning into stone.

Petrification can occur in another way as well. Water may dissolve away animal or plant material. That material is replaced by the minerals in the water. This type of petrification is called replacement. Replacement produces an exact stone copy of the original animal or plant.

In the Petrified Forest of Arizona are some fossil trees that were created by replacement. Great stone logs up to 3 meters in diameter and more than 36 meters long lie in the Petrified Forest. Scientists suspect that the trees were knocked down by floods that swept over the land more than 200 million years ago. The remains of the trees—the fossil logs—show almost every detail of the once-living forest. For example, the patterns of growth rings in the trunks of many trees show up so clearly that scientists can count the growth rings and determine how long the trees lived.

Molds and Casts

Two types of fossils are formed when an animal or a plant is buried in sediments that harden into rock. If the soft parts of the organism decay and the hard parts are dissolved by chemicals, an empty space will be left in the rock. The empty space, called a **mold**, has the same shape as the organism.

Sometimes the mold is filled in by minerals in the sediment. The minerals harden to form a **cast,** or filled-in mold. The cast is in the same shape as the original organism.

Imprints

Sometimes a fossil is formed before the sediments harden into rock. Thin objects—such as leaves and feathers—leave **imprints,** or impressions, in soft sediments such as mud. When the sediments harden into rock, the imprints are preserved as fossils.

One particular imprint fossil has provided scientists with a clue to the development of the first

birds. The imprint shows that the bird's skeleton was like that of a reptile with a toothed beak. Why do scientists believe the imprint was made by an ancient bird? The imprint also shows feathers around the skeleton, and only birds have feathers.

Figure 1–4 *Molds, casts, and imprints are types of fossils. Which part of the fossil shell is the mold? Which is the cast? The wing and tail feathers of this ancient bird are imprinted around its fossilized bones.*

Preservation of Entire Organisms

Perhaps the most spectacular kinds of fossils are those in which the whole body, or complete sections of it, is preserved. Although it is quite rare for both the soft and the hard parts of an organism to be preserved, some entire-organism fossils exist. How was the decay of these organisms stopped completely so that they could be preserved?

FREEZING   You probably know that freezing substances helps to preserve them. Freezing prevents substances from decaying. On occasion, scientists have found animals that have been preserved through freezing. Several extinct (no longer living on Earth) elephantlike animals called woolly mammoths have been discovered frozen in large blocks of ice. Woolly mammoths lived some 10,000 years ago. Another extinct animal, the furry rhinoceros, has been found preserved in the loose frozen soil in the arctic. So well preserved are the woolly mammoths and the furry rhinoceroses that wolves had sometimes eaten parts of the flesh when the ice had thawed.

ACTIVITY
WRITING

Terrible Lizards

Using reference materials in the library, look up information about these reptiles:
Brachiosaurus
Ankylosaurus
Plesiosaurus
Write a report that includes a description of each reptile and its habitat. Accompany your description with a drawing.

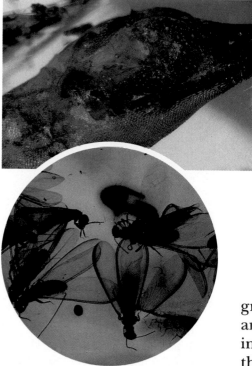

Figure 1–5 *Fossils may form when living things are trapped in tree resin that later hardens into amber. The tiny scales of the lizard, the hairlike bristles on the cricket's hind legs, and the delicate wings of the termites are perfectly preserved.*

AMBER When the resin (sap) from certain evergreen trees hardens, it forms a hard substance called amber. Flies and other insects are sometimes trapped in the sticky resin that flows from these trees. When the resin hardens, the insects are preserved in the amber. Insects found trapped in amber are usually perfectly preserved.

TAR PITS Tar pits are large pools of tar. Tar pits contain the fossil remains of many different animals. The animals were trapped in the sticky tar when they went to drink the water that often covered the pits. Other animals came to feed on the trapped animals and were also trapped in the tar. Eventually, the trapped animals sank to the bottom of the tar pits. Bison, camels, giant ground sloths, wolves, vultures, and saber-toothed cats are some of the animals found as fossils in the tar pits. In the La Brea tar pits in present-day Los Angeles, California, the complete skeletons of animals that lived more than a million years ago are perfectly preserved.

Most of the fossils recovered from tar pits are bones. The flesh of the trapped animals had either decayed or been eaten before the animals could be preserved. But whole furry rhinoceroses have been found in tar pits in Poland.

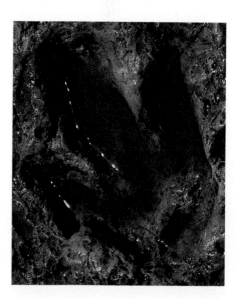

Figure 1–6 *Dinosaur footprints are an example of trace fossils. What are some other types of trace fossils? Why are such fossils important to scientists?*

Trace Fossils

Trace fossils are fossils that reveal much about an animal's appearance without showing any part of the animal. Trace fossils are the marks or evidence of animal activities. Tracks, trails, footprints, and burrows are trace fossils. Trace fossils can be left behind by animals such as worms, which are too soft to be otherwise preserved.

Interpreting Fossils

Scientists can learn a great deal about Earth's past from fossils. **Fossils indicate that many different life forms have existed at different times throughout Earth's history.** In fact, some scientists believe that for every type of organism living today, there are at least 100 types of organisms that have become extinct.

When fossils are arranged according to age, they show that living things have **evolved,** or changed over time. By examining the changes in fossils of a particular type of living thing, scientists can determine how that living thing has evolved over many millions of years. You will learn a good deal more about the process of evolution in Chapter 2.

Fossils also indicate how the Earth's surface has evolved. For example, if scientists find fossils of sea organisms in rocks high above sea level, they can assume that the land was once covered by an ocean.

Fossils also give scientists clues to Earth's past climate. For example, fossils of coral have been found in arctic regions. Coral is an animal that lives only in warm ocean areas. So evidence of the presence of coral in arctic regions indicates that the climate in the Arctic was once much warmer than it is today. Fossils of alligators similar to those found in Florida today have been located as far north as Canada. What kind of climate might once have existed when these fossils were living?

Fossils also tell scientists about the appearance and activities of extinct animals. From fossils of footprints, bones, and teeth, scientists construct models of extinct animals. They can even tell how big or heavy the animals were. Fossil footprints provide a clue as to how fast a particular animal could move.

Figure 1–7 *Scientists can learn much about the Earth's past from fossils. Although today's alligators live only in warm climates, alligatorlike fossils have been found as far north as Canada. What does this suggest about the past climate of Canada? What do the fossil shark teeth from a desert of Morocco indicate about that area's past? What characteristics of the shark's teeth indicate that it was a meat-eater?*

Although we may think of dinosaurs as being slow and plodding creatures, fossil footprints indicate that some dinosaurs could run as fast as 50 kilometers per hour. Fossils of teeth provide clues about the kind of food the animals ate. How might the shape of a tooth help scientists determine if an animal ate plants or other animals?

1–1 Section Review

1. What is a fossil? List five different types and describe how each forms.
2. Do molds and casts represent the remains of organisms or evidence of those organisms? Explain.
3. How can fossils provide evidence of climate changes on Earth?

Critical Thinking—*Applying Concepts*
4. The Hawaiian Islands are volcanic in origin. Would you expect to find many fossils of ancient Hawaiian organisms on the islands?

Guide for Reading

Focus on these questions as you read.

▶ *How do scientists use the law of superposition to determine the relative ages of rocks and fossils?*

▶ *How does the half-life of a radioactive element enable scientists to determine the absolute age of rocks and fossils?*

1–2 A History in Rocks and Fossils

Using evidence from rocks and fossils, scientists can determine the order of events that occurred in the past: what happened first, second, third, and so on. And scientists can often approximate the time at which the events happened. In other words, scientists can "write" a history of Earth.

One way to think of Earth's history is to picture a very large book filled with many pages. Each page tells the story of an event in the past. The stories of the earliest events are in the beginning pages; the stories of later events are in the pages near the end.

Although you could tell from such a book which events occurred before others, you could not know when the events occurred. In other words, you could tell the order of the events, but not their dates. To know when an event occurred, you would need numbers on the pages. If each number stood for a certain period of time—one million years perhaps—then you would have a fairly accurate calendar of Earth's history. As it turns out, scientists have both kinds of "history books" of Earth—one without page numbers but with a known order of pages, and one with page numbers as well.

The Law of Superposition

How, you might wonder, can scientists determine what events in Earth's history occurred before or after other events? That is, how do scientists develop their "book without dates"?

As you have read, most fossils are found in sedimentary rocks. Sedimentary rocks are made of layers of sediments that have piled up one atop the other. If the sediments have been left untouched, then clearly the layers of rocks at the bottom are older than those at the top. Put another way, the sedimentary layers are stacked in order of their age.

The **law of superposition** states that in a series of sedimentary rock layers, younger rocks normally lie on top of older rocks. The word superposition means one thing placed on top of another.

The law of superposition is based on the idea that sediments have been deposited in the same way throughout Earth's history. This idea was first proposed by the Scottish scientist James Hutton in the late eighteenth century. Hutton theorized that the processes acting on Earth's surface today are the same processes that have acted on Earth's surface in the past. These processes include weathering, erosion, and deposition. Weathering is the breaking down of rocks into sediments. Erosion is the carrying away of sediments. Deposition is the laying down of sediments.

Scientists use the law of superposition to determine whether a fossil or a layer of rock is older or younger than another fossil or layer of rock. Think of the layers of sedimentary rocks as the unnumbered pages of the "history book" that you have just read about. Remember, the beginning pages hold stories of long ago, while the end pages hold more recent stories. Now think of the words on each page as being a fossil. The words (fossil) on an earlier page (layer of rock) are older than the words (fossil) on a later page (layer of rock).

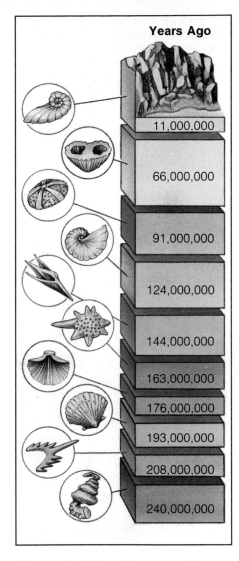

Years Ago

11,000,000

66,000,000

91,000,000

124,000,000

144,000,000

163,000,000

176,000,000

193,000,000

208,000,000

240,000,000

Figure 1–8 *Fossils are usually found in sedimentary rocks. If the sedimentary rock layers are in the same positions in which they formed, lower layers are older than upper ones. This principle is known as the law of superposition. How old are the fossils in the bottom layer of the diagram? The top layer?*

Figure 1–9 *The law of superposition helps scientists to determine the sequence of changes in life forms on the Earth. Is the spiral shell fossil older or younger than the cone-shaped shell fossil? How can you tell?*

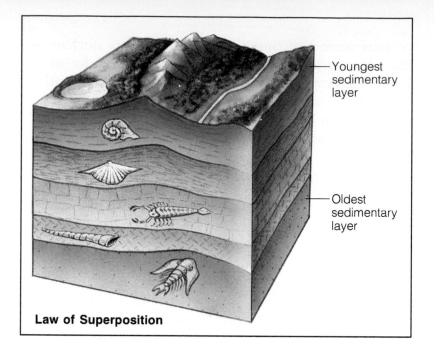

Youngest sedimentary layer

Oldest sedimentary layer

Law of Superposition

The process of sedimentation still occurs today. As you read these words, the fossils of tomorrow are being trapped in the sediments at the bottoms of rivers, lakes, and seas. For example, the Mississippi River deposits sediments at a rate of 80,000 tons an hour—day after day, year after year—at the point where the river flows into the Gulf of Mexico.

Index Fossils

The law of superposition helps scientists put in order the record of Earth's past for one particular location. But how can scientists get a worldwide picture of Earth's past? Is there a way of using the knowledge about the ages of rock layers in one location to find the relative ages of rock layers in other parts of the world? The relative age of an object is its age compared to the age of another object. Relative age does not provide dates for events, but it does provide a sequence of events.

In the early 1800s, scientists working on opposite sides of the English Channel came up with a way to determine relative ages of rock layers in different parts of the world. The scientists were digging through layers of sedimentary rocks near the southern coast of England and the northern coast of France. In both locations, the scientists discovered fossils of sea-dwelling shellfish. Clearly, both coasts had been under water at some time in the past.

ACTIVITY

WRITING

Index Fossils

Index fossils are used to identify the age of sedimentary rock layers. Using reference materials from the library, find out the names of several index fossils. Identify the period during which the fossilized organisms lived. Present your findings in a written report.

As you can see from Figure 1–10, four distinct kinds of shellfish fossils were found on both sides of the channel. Fossil 1 was found only in the upper layers. Fossil 2 was found in various layers. Fossil 3 was found only in middle layers. And fossil 4 was found only in the lower layers. Because the same fossils were found in similar rock layers on both sides of the channel, the scientists concluded that layers with the same fossils were the same age. Thus fossils 1, 3, and 4 were clues to the relative ages of the rock layers. Fossil 2 was not. Explain why.

Fossils such as fossils 1, 3, and 4 in Figure 1–10 are called **index fossils.** Index fossils are fossils of organisms that lived during only one short period of time. Scientists assume that index fossils of the same type of organism are all nearly the same age. So a layer of rock with one type of index fossil in it is close in age to another layer of rock with the same type of index fossil in it. Even though the rock layers may be in different regions of the world, the index fossils indicate that the layers are close in age. Why would the fossil of an organism that lived for a long period of time not be a good index fossil?

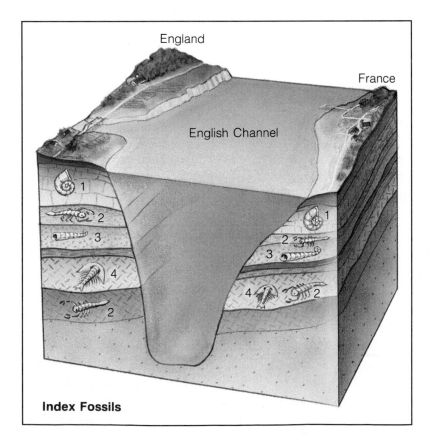

Index Fossils

Figure 1–10 *Index fossils are fossils of organisms that lived during only one short period of time. This illustration shows the rock layers on both sides of the English Channel. Even though the rock layers are separated by about 30 kilometers, there are three kinds of index fossils that are found on both sides. So scientists concluded that the English rock layers were the same age as the French rock layers that contain the same index fossils. Which three fossils helped scientists to reach this conclusion? Which fossil cannot be used to determine the relative age of the English and French rock layers?*

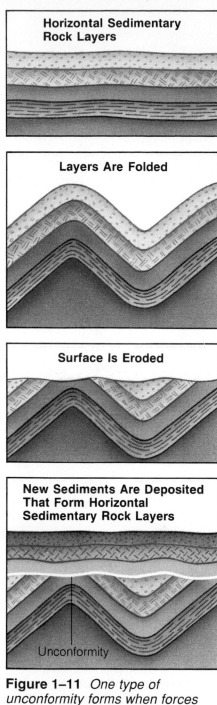

Horizontal Sedimentary Rock Layers

Layers Are Folded

Surface Is Eroded

New Sediments Are Deposited That Form Horizontal Sedimentary Rock Layers

Unconformity

Figure 1–11 *One type of unconformity forms when forces within the Earth fold and tilt previously horizontal sedimentary rock layers (top and top center). In time, the layers are worn down to almost a flat surface (bottom center). After a long period of time, new rock layers form, covering the old surface and producing an unconformity (bottom).*

Unconformities

Sedimentary rock layers and the fossils found within them may be disturbed by powerful forces within the Earth. The rock layers may be folded, bent, and twisted. Sometimes older, deeply buried layers of rocks are uplifted to the Earth's surface. At the surface, the exposed rocks are weathered and eroded. Sediments are then deposited on top of the eroded surface of the older rocks. The deposited sediments harden to form new horizontal sedimentary rock layers. The old eroded surface beneath the newer rock layers is called an **unconformity.** Tilted sedimentary rock layers covered by younger horizontal sedimentary layers is an example of an unconformity. See Figure 1–11.

There is a wide gap in the ages of the rock layers above and below an unconformity. There is also a wide gap in the ages of the fossils in these rock layers. By studying unconformities, scientists can tell where and when the Earth's crust has undergone changes such as tilting, uplifting, and erosion. In addition, scientists can learn about the effects of these changes on the organisms living at that time.

Faults, Intrusions, and Extrusions

There are other clues to the relative ages of rocks and the history of events on Earth. During movements of the Earth's crust, rocks may break or crack. A break or crack along which rocks move is called a **fault.** The rock layers on one side of a fault may shift up or down relative to the rock layers on the other side of the fault.

Because faults can occur only after rock layers are formed, rock layers are always older than the faults they contain. The relative age of a fault can be determined from the relative age of the sedimentary layer that the fault cuts across. Scientists can determine the forces that have changed the Earth's surface by examining the faults in rock layers.

The relative ages of igneous rock formations can also be determined. Magma often forces its way into layers of rocks. The magma hardens in the rock layers and forms an **intrusion.** An intrusion is younger than the sedimentary rock layers it passes through.

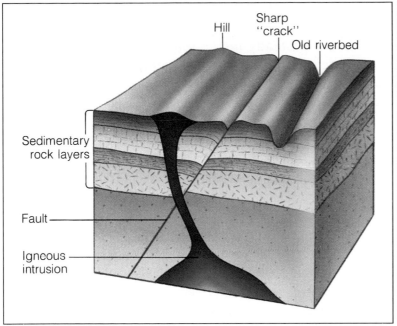

Figure 1–12 *Intrusions of igneous rock may be exposed when the overlying rock has been worn away. The diagram shows how intrusions and faults affect the arrangement of the rocks in an area.*

Sometimes magma reaches the surface of the Earth as lava and hardens. Igneous rock that forms on the Earth's surface is called an **extrusion.** Extrusions are younger than the rock layers beneath them. What do extrusions tell scientists about the Earth's past?

A History With Dates

By the end of the nineteenth century, scientists had developed a clear picture of Earth's past as recorded by fossils and rocks. The picture showed great and varied changes. The continents had changed shape many times. High mountains had risen and had been worn away to hills. Life had begun in the sea and had later moved onto land. Living things had evolved through many stages to the forms that exist today. Climates around the world had also changed many times.

Scientists knew that these changes had taken place. They knew the order in which the changes had happened. But what they did not know was how many years the changes had taken. How many years ago had each event happened? It seemed clear that all the changes had taken a lot of time—certainly millions of years. But could a clock made of rock layers measure such lengths of time?

Figure 1–13 *The formation and wearing away of sedimentary rock layers do not occur at steady rates throughout geologic history. These rocks on the coast of New Zealand may have been built faster and worn away slower—or vice versa—than they were elsewhere. And the rates at which the rocks were built and destroyed may have varied greatly over time.*

To create a clock to measure time, you need to have a series of events that take place at a steady rate, like the steady movement of the second hand on a watch. The first clock developed by scientists to measure Earth's age was the rate at which sedimentary rock is deposited.

The scientists decided to assume that sediment was deposited at a steady rate throughout Earth's past. That rate, they reasoned, should be the same as it is in the present. Let's say the rate is 30 millimeters per century (100 years). If the total depth of sedimentary rocks deposited since the depositing began was measured and then divided by the yearly rate, the age of the oldest sedimentary rock could be calculated. In fact, this method could be used to determine the age of any sedimentary rock layer—and the fossils it contained.

In 1899, a British scientist used this method and came up with a maximum age for sedimentary rocks of about 75 million years. Although in some parts of the world this dating system seemed to work fairly well, it was not actually an accurate method of measuring time. Its greatest drawback was that there is not, and never has been, such a thing as a steady rate of deposition. A flood of the Mississippi River can lay down two meters of muddy sediment in a single day. But hundreds of years may pass before one meter of mud piles up at the bottom of a lake or pond.

So using the deposition of sediments to determine the age of Earth is like trying to use a clock that runs at widely different rates. Nevertheless, the invention of this "sedimentary clock" marked the beginning of efforts to measure the absolute age of events on Earth. Absolute age gives the precise time an event occurred, not just the order of events that relative age provides.

By the beginning of the twentieth century scientists who study the history and structure of the Earth agreed that Earth was at least several hundred million years old. Today, scientists know Earth's age to be about 4.6 billion years. What kind of clock do scientists use to measure the Earth's age so accurately? Strange as it may seem, the clock they use is a radioactive clock!

Radioactive Dating

The discovery of radioactive elements in 1896 led to the development of an accurate method of determining the absolute age of rocks and fossils. An atom of a radioactive element has an unstable nucleus, or center, that breaks down, or decays. During radioactive decay, particles and energy called radiation are released by the radioactive element.

As some radioactive elements decay, they form decay elements. A decay element is the stable element into which a radioactive element breaks down. **The breakdown of a radioactive element into a decay element occurs at a constant rate.** Some radioactive elements decay in a few seconds. Some take thousands, millions, or even billions of years to decay. But no matter how long it takes for an element to decay, the rate of decay for that element is absolutely steady. No force known can either speed it up or slow it down.

Scientists measure the decay rate of a radioactive element by a unit called **half-life.** The half-life of an element is the time it takes for half of the radioactive element to decay.

For example, if you begin with 1 kilogram of a radioactive element, half of that kilogram will decay during one half-life. So at the end of one half-life, you will have 0.50 kilograms of the radioactive element and 0.50 kilograms of the decay element. Half of the remaining element (half of a half) will decay during another half-life. At this point one quarter of the radioactive element remains. How much of the decay element is there? This process continues until all the radioactive element has decayed. Figure 1–15 on page 26 illustrates the decay of a radioactive element with a half-life of 1 billion years.

If certain radioactive elements are present in a rock or fossil, scientists can find the absolute age of the rock or fossil. For example, suppose a rock contains a radioactive element that has a half-life of 1 million years. If tests show that the rock contains

Figure 1–14 *A knowledge of life science was needed to correctly reassemble the tiny bones in the skeleton of a hatching dinosaur. How does a knowledge of physical science help a scientist to determine the absolute age of the fossil?*

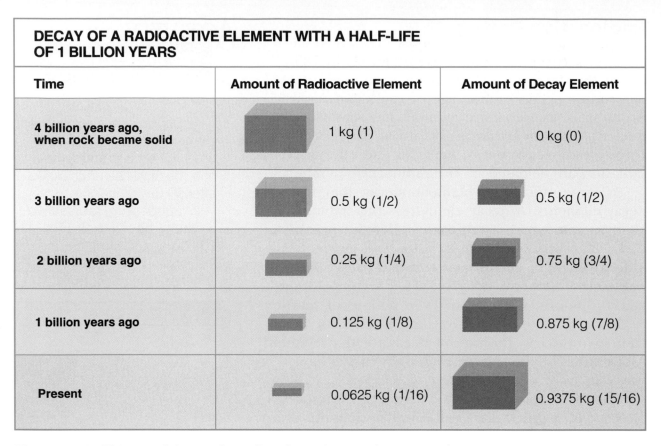

DECAY OF A RADIOACTIVE ELEMENT WITH A HALF-LIFE OF 1 BILLION YEARS

Time	Amount of Radioactive Element	Amount of Decay Element
4 billion years ago, when rock became solid	1 kg (1)	0 kg (0)
3 billion years ago	0.5 kg (1/2)	0.5 kg (1/2)
2 billion years ago	0.25 kg (1/4)	0.75 kg (3/4)
1 billion years ago	0.125 kg (1/8)	0.875 kg (7/8)
Present	0.0625 kg (1/16)	0.9375 kg (15/16)

Figure 1–15 *The rate of decay of a radioactive substance is measured by its half-life. How much of the radioactive element remains after 2 billion years?*

equal amounts of the radioactive element and its decay element, the rock is about 1 million years old. Since the proportion of radioactive element to decay element is equal, the element has gone through only one half-life. Scientists use the proportion of radioactive element to decay element to determine how many half-lives have occurred. If the rock contains three times as much decay element as it does radioactive element, how many half-lives have occurred? How old is the rock?

Many different radioactive elements are used to date rocks and fossils. Figure 1–16 lists some radioactive elements and their half-lives. One radioactive element used to date the remains of living things is carbon-14. Carbon-14 is present in all living things. It can be used to date fossils such as wood, bones, and shells that were formed within the last 50,000 years. It is difficult to measure the amount of

HALF-LIVES OF ELEMENTS USED TO FIND THE AGE OF ROCKS AND FOSSILS

Element	Half-life	Used to Find Age of
Rubidium-87	50.00 billion years	Very old rocks
Thorium-232	13.90 billion years	Very old rocks
Uranium-238	4.51 billion years	Old rocks and fossils in them
Potassium-40	1.30 billion years	Old rocks and fossils in them
Uranium-235	713 million years	Old rocks and fossils in them
Carbon-14	5730 years	Fossils (usually no older than about 50,000 years)

Figure 1–16 *Each radioactive substance has a different half-life. These substances are used to measure the age of different rocks and fossils. What is the half-life of potassium-40? Can you explain why carbon-14 is not used to determine the age of dinosaur fossils?*

carbon-14 in a rock or fossil more than 50,000 years old because almost all of the carbon-14 will have decayed into nitrogen. Nitrogen is the decay element of carbon-14. Using the information in Figure 1–16, which radioactive elements would you choose to date a fossil or rock found in the oldest rocks on Earth?

The Age of the Earth

Scientists use radioactive dating to help determine the age of rocks. By finding the age of rocks, they can estimate the age of the Earth. Scientists have found some rocks in South Africa that are more than 4 billion years old—the oldest rocks found on the Earth so far.

Radioactive dating of moon rocks brought back by the Apollo missions shows them to be 4 to 4.6 billion years old. The oldest moon rocks, then, are more than a half billion years older than the oldest known Earth rocks. However, because scientists have evidence that the Earth and the moon formed at the same time, they believe that the Earth is about 4.6 billion years old.

PROBLEM Solving

People-Eating Dinosaurs?

As the world's leading expert on fossils, you have been called upon to resolve a growing controversy. Recently, a collection of human bones have been found at the mouth of an ancient river. Grooves on the bones show that they were chewed by a large animal. Near the bones were discovered the tracks of a meat-eating dinosaur. Newspapers throughout the world have declared the find as evidence that people and dinosaurs once lived together and that the dinosaurs hunted and ate people. However, as a scientist, you know that the dinosaurs were extinct for over 60 million years before the first humans evolved on Earth.

Interpreting Evidence

1. What tests would you perform to demonstrate that the humans were not eaten by dinosaurs?

2. What other hypothesis can you provide to explain the find?

1–2 Section Review

1. How is the law of superposition used to date fossils?
2. Do index fossils provide evidence for relative age or absolute age? Explain.
3. Compare an intrusion and an extrusion.
4. How do scientists use the half-life of a radioactive element to date rocks and fossils?

Connection—*You and Your World*

5. While digging in her backyard, Carmela finds the bones of a fish. Carmela immediately decides that the bones provide evidence that the area she lives in was once under water. Is Carmela correct in her analysis or could there be some other explanation for her findings?

1–3 A Trip Through Geologic Time

The Earth's clock began ticking long ago. So long ago that the major units of time of this clock could not be seconds, hours, days, weeks, months, or even years. There would be just too many of these units for them to be useful in setting up a calendar of Earth's history. For example, more than 1.5 trillion days have passed since Earth formed. If each of these days took up one page of an ordinary office calendar, the calendar would be about 140,000 kilometers thick. Not very practical—and a bit difficult to carry around.

In order to divide geologic time into workable units, scientists have established the geologic time scale. **Earth's history on the geologic time scale is divided into four geologic eras: Precambrian Era, Paleozoic Era, Mesozoic Era, and Cenozoic Era.** An era is the largest division of the geologic time scale. Eras are broken into smaller subdivisions called periods.

The eras of Earth's geologic time scale are of different lengths. Geologic time is the length of time Earth has existed. The Precambrian (pree-KAM-bree-uhn) Era is the longest era. It lasted about 4 billion years and accounts for about 87 percent of Earth's history. The Paleozoic (pay-lee-oh-ZOH-ihk) Era

Guide for Reading

Focus on these questions as you read.

▶ *What are the four geologic eras?*

▶ *What were the major life forms and geologic events during the four geologic eras?*

Figure 1–17 *Many unusual animals lived long ago, such as the meat-eating saber-toothed cat (top) and the plant-eating dinosaur (bottom).*

GEOLOGIC HISTORY OF THE EARTH

Era	Precambrian	Paleozoic			
Began (millions of years ago)	4600	570			
Ended (millions of years ago)	570	225			
Length (millions of years)	4030	345			
Period	None	**Cambrian**	**Ordovician**	**Silurian**	**Devonian**
Began (millions of years ago)	4600	570	500	430	395
Ended (millions of years ago)	570	500	430	395	345
Length (millions of years)	4030	70	70	35	50
	Earth's history begins; seas form; mountains begin to grow; oxygen builds up in atmosphere; first life forms in sea; as time passes, bacteria, algae, jellyfish, corals, and clams develop	Shallow seas cover parts of continents; many trilobites, brachiopods, sponges, and other sea-living invertebrates are present	Many volcanoes and mountains form; North America is flooded; first fish (jawless) appear; invertebrates flourish in the sea	Caledonian Mountains of Scandinavia rise; coral reefs form; first land plants, air-breathing animals, and jawed fish develop	Acadian Mountains of New York rise; erosion of mountains deposits much sediment in seas; first forests grow in swampy areas; first amphibians, sharks, and insects develop

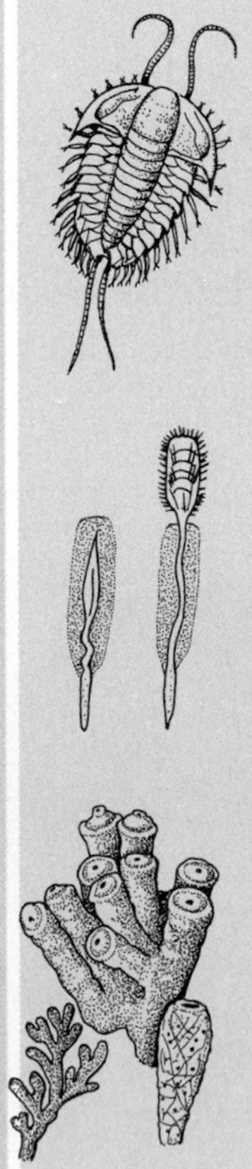

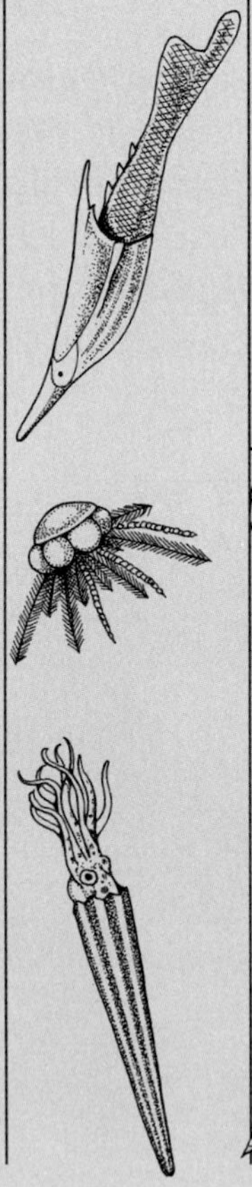

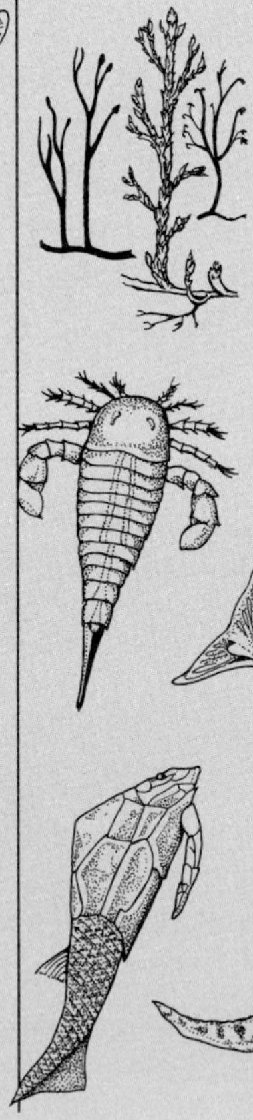

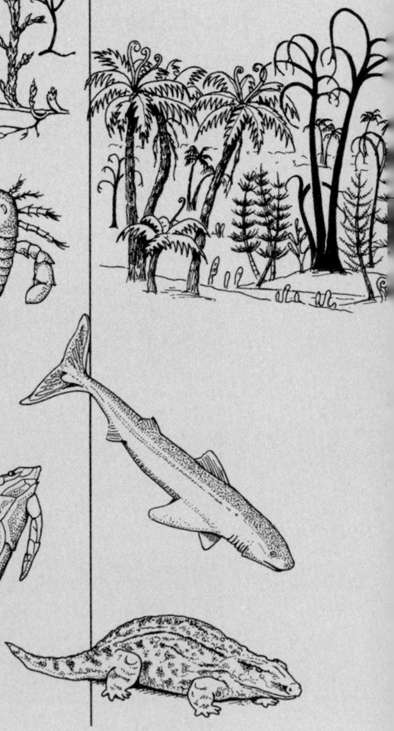

Figure 1–18 *This chart illustrates the geologic history of the Earth. What events occurred during the Permian Period? When did modern humans appear?*

		Mesozoic			Cenozoic	
		225			65	
		65			The present	
		160			65	

*In North America, the Carboniferous Period is often subdivided into the Mississippian Period (345–310 million years ago) and the Pennsylvanian Period (310–280 million years ago).

Carboniferous*	Permian	Triassic	Jurassic	Cretaceous	Tertiary	Quaternary
345	280	225	190	136	65	1.8
280	225	190	136	65	1.8	The present
65	55	35	54	71	63.2	1.8
Appalachian Mountains of North America form; ice covers large areas of the Earth; swamps cover lowlands; first mosses, reptiles, and winged insects appear; great coal-forming forests form; seed-bearing ferns grow	Ural Mountains of Russia rise; first cone-bearing plants appear; ferns, fish, amphibians, and reptiles flourish; many sea-living invertebrates, including trilobites, die out	Palisades of New Jersey and Caucasus Mountains of Russia form; first dinosaurs and first mammals appear; modern corals, modern fish, and modern insect types develop	The Rocky Mountains rise; volcanoes of North American West are active; first birds appear; palms and cone-bearing trees flourish; largest dinosaurs thrive; primitive mammals develop	First flowering plants appear; placental mammals develop; dinosaurs die out, as do many sea-living reptiles	Andes, Alps, and Himalayan Mountains rise; first horses, primates, and humanlike creatures develop; flowering plants thrive; mammals take on present-day features	Ice covers large parts of North America and Europe; Great Lakes form as ice melts; first modern human beings appear; woolly mammoths die out; civilization begins

Figure 1–19 *Many volcanic eruptions occurred during the early geologic history of the Earth.*

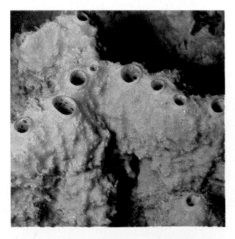

Figure 1–20 *Modern sponges are quite similar to their earliest ancestors, which appeared at the end of the Precambrian Era.*

lasted about 345 million years, and the Mesozoic (mehs-oh-ZOH-ihk) Era about 160 million years. The Cenozoic (see-nuh-ZOH-ihk) Era, the era in which we now live, has lasted for only 65 million years. To get a better understanding of these eras and the events that occurred during each one, you will now take a short imaginary trip through Earth's history.

The Precambrian Era: The Dawn of Life

You begin your trip in space, gazing upon planet Earth from a safe distance. The time is 4.6 billion years ago, and Earth is a planet of molten rock much too hot to set foot upon. The atmosphere, unlike today's atmosphere, contains mainly poisonous gases. Because of widespread volcanic eruptions and cooling and hardening of lava, there is no record in the rocks from this distant time.

Skip ahead in your mind about 1.5 billion years later. The Earth is cooler now. Continents and oceans have formed. Although the air is warm and quite humid, little oxygen exists in the atmosphere. In fact, much of the atmosphere contains sulfur dioxide gas that has been released by volcanic eruptions. It is a dynamic and restless time in Earth's history.

Gazing down on the shores of a Precambrian sea, you notice a rocky shoreline with no signs of life. The scene is the same all over Earth. Rain falls and thunder rolls. But on land there are no plants to receive the rain and no animals to hear the thunder. Nor will there be for the next 2.6 billion years!

But there is life in the seas. If you look closely you will see faint signs of it. Lying on rocks just beneath the sea surface are patches of what looks like mold. The patches are several centimeters across. They are made of millions of bacteria clumped together in a tangled mat of threadlike fibers. Billions of years later scientists will find fossils of these bacteria—the oldest fossils ever found.

Plants related to modern seaweed are in the seas as well. They use simple chemicals in the water plus energy from sunlight to make their own food, just as green plants have done ever since. In the process, they produce oxygen. Over the next billion years, more and more oxygen will dissolve in the sea water and enter the atmosphere. Animal life will become possible.

By the end of the Precambrian Era, animals such as jellyfish and worms have appeared in the seas, along with sponges and corals. Although sponges and corals look like plants, they are actually colonies of animal cells.

The Paleozoic Era: Life Comes Ashore

Your imaginary trip has brought you to the Paleozoic Era. The time is 570 million years ago, and even a quick glance alerts you to the fact that the land is still lifeless. But life is abundant in the seas. Worms of many kinds crawl across the sandy bottom. Strange "plants," which seem to grow from the sea floor, resemble animal horns, vases, and bells. These formations are actually sponges.

Parts of the sea floor contain lampshade-shaped shells. The shells have two parts that close to cover and protect the soft animal within. These animals are brachiopods.

Other sea animals have large heads, long thorny spines, and many body divisions. They have jointed legs like those of a modern insect or lobster. These animals are trilobites. They will become an important index fossil for the Paleozoic Era. They evolved rapidly during that era, leaving different forms in

Figure 1–21 *Brachiopods were quite common during the Paleozoic Era—about 30,000 species are known from their fossil shells. Although brachiopods look somewhat like clams, they are as distantly related to clams as you are.*

Figure 1–22 *Strange armored fishes swam in the waters during the Devonian Period. What is this period's nickname?*

Figure 1–23 *Creatures of the Paleozoic seas included starfish (top) and trilobites (center and bottom). This starfish is unusual because it has six arms, whereas most modern starfish have five. Why are trilobites important index fossils?*

each of the era's periods, and then became extinct by the era's end.

The seas are truly teeming with life. Fishes can be found almost everywhere. Fishes are the first vertebrates, or animals with backbones, to appear on Earth. In fact, the Devonian period, one of the periods of the Paleozoic Era, is often called the Age of Fishes.

By the end of the Paleozoic Era, the land is no longer lifeless. Huge forests of ferns have developed. There are also cycads, which are trees with a crown of fernlike leaves. Cycads are among the first seed plants. In the future, the sago palm, one of the few modern cycads, will be called a living fossil. Scientists believe that the remains of these forests of ferns and other plants formed the huge coal deposits in the United States and other parts of the world.

Amphibians, such as *Eryops,* now appear as well. Amphibians are the first land vertebrates. The name amphibian, which means "living a double life," is quite appropriate, since amphibians typically spend their early lives in water and then move to land. *Eryops* is a far larger amphibian than its twentieth-century relatives, such as frogs and toads. It is almost 2 meters long, with a large head and a thick, clumsy body. *Eryops* waddles through the forest in search of king-sized roaches and other tasty meals. But because *Eryops* must keep its skin moist in order to survive, it does not move far from water.

By the end of the Paleozoic Era, the amphibians have run up against hard times. There is drought, and the climate has cooled. Mountains are rising in what will become Norway, Scotland, Greenland, and parts of North America. These areas, as well as all the other landmasses on Earth, are joined together as one single continent. Scientists will one day call this continent Pangaea, but that is still about 225 million years in the future.

New kinds of animals that live on land all the time are appearing. Their tough skin is protected by scales or hard plates. Unlike amphibians, these animals do not lose water through their skins. Their eggs have thick shells, so the eggs do not dry out. The animals are reptiles, and for the next 160 million years they will dominate Earth.

Figure 1–24 *Amphibians evolved from fish ancestors during the Paleozoic Era. Like typical amphibians,* Eryops *lived in water when it was young. As an adult, this ancient amphibian lived in moist places on land.*

The Mesozoic Era: Mammals Develop

Your trip continues as you enter the Mesozoic Era, which began about 225 million years ago. The Mesozoic Era is a period of many changes—both in the land and in the living things that inhabit Earth. Scientists believe that Pangaea began to break apart during the Mesozoic Era. The expansion of the ocean floor along midocean ridges caused the continents gradually to spread apart. Midocean ridges are chains of underwater volcanic mountains. Today the continents are still moving apart at the midocean ridges.

As Pangaea broke apart, there were numerous earthquakes and volcanic eruptions. Many mountains were formed at this time. The Appalachian Mountains were leveled by erosion during the early part of the Mesozoic Era. Then they were uplifted again late in the era. The Sierra Nevada and Rocky Mountains were formed during the late stages of the Mesozoic Era.

Scientists divide the Mesozoic Era into three periods. The oldest period is called the Triassic (trigh-AS-ihk) Period. The middle period is called the Jurassic (joo-RAS-ihk) Period. The youngest period is called the Cretaceous (krih-TAY-shuhs) Period.

ACTIVITY READING

Good Mother Lizard

If you think that dinosaurs were slow-witted, slow moving creatures, you will be in for a surprise if you read *Maia—A Dinosaur Grows Up* by Jack Horner. In this book you will discover what it might have been like to be an infant dinosaur in a world with so many ferocious creatures.

Figure 1–25 *Reptiles dominated the land, sky, and seas during the Mesozoic Era. Porpoiselike ichthyosaurs and long-necked plesiosaurs swam swiftly through the oceans in search of food.*

ACTIVITY

DOING

Pangaea

Fossils of the same land animals have been found on separate continents. Scientists say such findings are evidence that at one time Earth had one supercontinent called Pangaea.

Using materials in the library, find out which fossil animals support the idea of Pangaea. Write down the names of the fossil animals and where they were discovered on the continents.

Mark off these discovery sites on a world map. At which points do you think the continents came together?

THE TRIASSIC PERIOD As you enter the Triassic Period you notice that the drought that began in the Paleozoic Era has not ended. The climate, in fact, is even hotter than before. Slowly, very slowly, you see North and South America begin to separate from Africa. A narrow sea opens between North America and what is now Iceland and England. This sea will become the North Atlantic Ocean. The southern lands of Africa, South America, Antarctica, and India are still joined.

In the seas, you spot creatures that are shaped like fish. But they are not fish. The bones in their fins have five fingerlike projections, like the limbs of land animals. They have lungs and breathe air. These creatures are reptiles—land-living animals—that have returned to the sea.

Mammals appear in the Triassic Period. Mammals are animals with hair or fur, whose offspring, for the most part, do not hatch from eggs. The young grow and mature in their mother's body before birth.

Ferns and seed ferns are still common. Cycads are growing bigger. During this time, the trees that will become the Petrified Forest of Arizona are uprooted by floods. The first dinosaurs are appearing. Many are small, no bigger than chickens. They have small heads, long tails, and walk on their hind legs.

THE JURASSIC PERIOD   As you move forward into the Jurassic Period, you notice that the dinosaurs that will be found at Bone Cabin Quarry have now appeared. The Age of Dinosaurs has begun. Volcanoes are active in the American West. The mountains of the Sierra Nevada and Rocky Mountain ranges are rising. The North Atlantic is still quite narrow. The southern continents, still closely linked, are just beginning to separate. Animals and plants are similar throughout this "supercontinent."

Huge cycads and modern-looking evergreens called conifers make up the forests. There are no flowers yet. Toward the end of the Jurassic Period, one of the first birds, Archaeopteryx (ahr-kee-AHP-ter-iks), appears. Its name means "ancient wing."

THE CRETACEOUS PERIOD   The Cretaceous Period is a time of widespread flooding of continents by seas. The continents continue moving apart. By the end of the period, they are pretty much as they are now, although North America and Europe are still joined.

Dinosaurs still dominate the world. *Tyrannosaurus,* the greatest meat eater of all times, stalks the land. Among the plant eaters are the armored *Triceratops* and the strange-looking duck-billed dinosaurs. By the end of the Cretacious Period, however, all the dinosaurs will have died out. So will the sea-living reptiles. Of all the different reptiles of the Mesozoic Era, only crocodiles, turtles, lizards, and snakes will have survived. The mysterious mass extinctions of so many forms of life will puzzle scientists of the future. The scientists will debate whether the extinctions were due to a change in climate, a worldwide disease, or even the result of a gigantic asteroid crashing into the Earth.

The Cretaceous Period was a time of rapid change—rapid, that is, in terms of Earth's long past. During this period, sea levels dropped. Rivers and flood plains, where many dinosaurs thrived, dried up. Flowering plants appeared—among them such familiar trees as magnolia, oak, fig, poplar, elm,

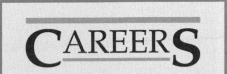

CAREERS

Museum Technician
People who prepare museum collections are called **museum technicians.** They clean and preserve animal and plant specimens and carefully mount and arrange them in glass cases. They also work with fossils that have been recently discovered, restoring the skeletal parts with the use of clay, plaster, and other materials.

Museum technicians require special skills at doing detailed work, so on-the-job training is important. For further career information, write to American Association of Museums, 1055 Thomas Jefferson St., NW, Washington, DC 20007.

Figure 1–26 *Dinosaurs were still masters of the land during the Cretaceous Period. But their reign was soon to come to an end.*

birch, and willow. As the new plant life spread and flourished, most of the great tree ferns and cycads died out. The world was beginning to take on a look that is much more familiar to you.

The Cenozoic Era: A World With People

You are about to enter the era that began approximately 65 million years ago—the era in which you live. The Cenozoic Era will be divided into two great periods known for the evolution of the first horses and the evolution of the first animals to walk on two feet. Great sheets of ice will sweep across the land. And finally, almost at the end of your trip through geologic time, a new kind of living thing will make its home on Earth and attempt to make sense of all that has passed.

THE TERTIARY PERIOD You find yourself near what will one day be the town of Green River, in southwest Wyoming, not too many kilometers from the site of Bone Cabin Quarry. It is about 50 million years ago. Although in many ways the land is familiar, there is something odd about it.

In a grassy meadow, you hear birds singing. There are groups of redwoods, oaks, and cedars. But there are groves of palm trees, too! Worldwide, the

climate is mild. And it will stay that way through most of this period.

Trotting through the meadow you see a beast that makes you wonder whether you are in Africa. It is about the size of an elephant, with elephantlike legs. Its skin is gray and wrinkled. Its tail, with a tuft of hair at the end, looks much like a lion's tail. But its head and ears are those of a rhinoceros. Instead of one or two horns, however, the animal has six horns.

The animal is *Uintatherium* (yoo-wihn-tuh-THEER-ee-uhm). The name means "Uinta beast," after the Uinta Mountains of Utah and Wyoming. Wandering the meadows with *Uintatherium* is a direct ancestor of the rhinoceros. It is no larger than a large dog. Another dog-sized animal, *Eohippus,* is the earliest horse.

Somewhere around 3.4 million years ago, toward the end of the Tertiary Period, humanlike creatures begin walking upright on the African plains. One is a small adult female about 1 meter tall. Scientists will find her skeleton in 1977. They will call her "Lucy."

THE QUATERNARY PERIOD The climate turns sharply colder during the Quaternary Period. On four different occasions, great sheets of ice advance from the Arctic and Antarctic regions, only to retreat

ACTIVITY
DOING

The Time of Your Life

1. On white index cards, write several important events that have happened to you in your life. *Place one event on each card.*

2. Arrange the cards in the order in which the events happened.

3. Using colored index cards, write one of the following on each: Preschool Years, Early Elementary School Years, Middle Elementary School Years, Late Elementary School Years, Junior High School/Middle School Years (if applicable). Insert each colored index card in front of the group of events that occurred during those years.

How does the arrangement of the cards resemble a geologic time line?

Figure 1–27 Uintatherium, *which lived during the beginning of the Tertiary Period, was one of the largest and strangest-looking mammals ever to walk the Earth.*

as the climate becomes milder. At their worst, these ice ages are like winters that last thousands of years. Large parts of Europe and North and South America are ice-covered. The last ice age ends about 11,000 years ago. As the world warms, farming becomes widespread and modern civilization begins.

Now it is time to end your trip and return home. What will happen in the Quaternary Period from this point on is modern history. The only way to find out is to wait and see.

Figure 1–28 *The weather became much cooler during the Quaternary Period. Sheets of ice repeatedly advanced and retreated over the Earth.*

1–3 Section Review

1. What are the four eras of geologic time?
2. In what era did the first vertebrates appear?
3. During what period did the first birds evolve?
4. Identify and describe one animal associated with each of the following eras: Paleozoic, Mesozoic, Cenozoic.
5. Why is it difficult to determine the geologic era to which an area of metamorphic rock belonged?

Critical Thinking—*Making Inferences*

6. How might the collision of a huge asteroid with Earth result in the extinction of the dinosaurs? *Hint:* Assume the dinosaurs were not killed by the impact alone.

CONNECTIONS

Breaking Up Is Hard to Do

While we tend to think of the continents as being somewhat timeless, you have read that the continents are much different today than they were in the past. The idea that continents are in motion, moving along on huge plates that make up Earth's crust, is called *plate tectonics.*

Scientists believe that some 250 million years ago, all the world's landmasses were contained in one supercontinent called Pangaea. But about 200 million years ago, Pangaea split into two large continents called Gondwanaland and Laurasia. As time passed, Gondwanaland split into three parts. One part consisted of South America and Africa. Another part consisted of Antarctica and Australia. The third part was India. More time passed, and India drifted north and collided with Asia. South America and Africa separated. Laurasia, the other continent, split apart to form North America and Eurasia. Australia broke away from Antarctica and slowly drifted to its current position.

The continents are still drifting today at a rate of about 1 to 5 centimeters per year. What might the Earth look like in another 100 million years?

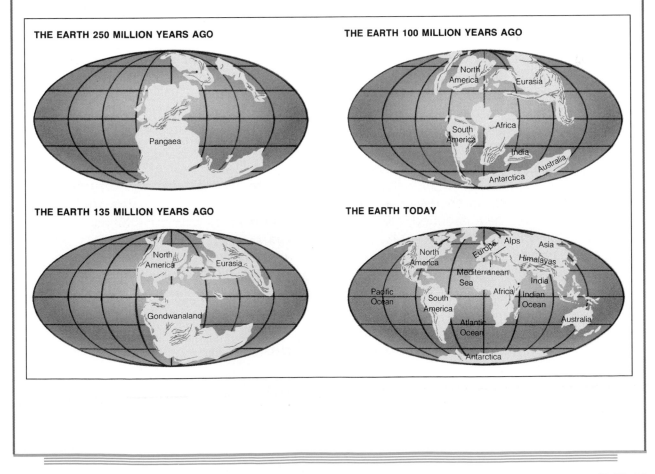

THE EARTH 250 MILLION YEARS AGO

Pangaea

THE EARTH 100 MILLION YEARS AGO

North America
Eurasia
South America
Africa
India
Australia
Antarctica

THE EARTH 135 MILLION YEARS AGO

North America
Eurasia
Gondwanaland

THE EARTH TODAY

North America
Europe
Alps
Asia
Himalayas
Mediterranean Sea
India
Pacific Ocean
Africa
Indian Ocean
South America
Atlantic Ocean
Australia
Antarctica

Laboratory Investigation

Interpreting Fossil Molds and Casts

Problem

What fossil evidence can be obtained from molds and casts?

Materials *(per group)*

small, empty milk carton
petroleum jelly
plaster of Paris
stirring rod or spoon
3 small objects

Procedure

1. Open completely the top of the empty milk container. Grease the inside of the container with petroleum jelly.

2. Mix the plaster of Paris, following the directions on the package. Pour the mixture into the milk container so that the container is half full.

3. Rub a coat of petroleum jelly over the objects you are going to use.

4. When the plaster of Paris begins to harden, gently press the objects into the plaster so that they are not entirely covered. After the mixture has hardened, carefully remove the objects. You should be able to see the imprints of your objects.

5. Coat the entire surface of the hardened plaster of Paris with petroleum jelly.

6. Mix more plaster of Paris. Pour it on top of the hardened plaster of Paris so that it fills the container. After the plaster hardens, tear the milk carton away from the plaster block. Gently pull the two layers of plaster apart. You now have a cast and a mold of the objects.

7. Exchange your molds and casts for those of another group. Number each cast and mold set from 1 to 3. In a chart, record the number of each set. Record your prediction of what object made each cast and mold.

8. Get the original objects from the other group and see if your predictions were correct. Record in your chart what the actual object is.

Observations

1. What are the similarities and differences between the casts and molds?

2. What are the similarities and differences between the casts and the original objects they were made from?

Number	Predicted Object	Actual Object

Analysis and Conclusions

1. Compare the formation of a plaster mold with the formation of a fossil mold.

2. Compare the way you predicted what the unknown object was with the way a scientist predicts what object left a fossil cast or mold.

3. **On Your Own** Find a set of prints or tracks left by an animal in concrete (such as a concrete sidewalk). Determine what the animal looked like, based on its "fossil" prints.

Summarizing Key Concepts

1–1 Fossils—Clues to the Past

▲ Fossils are the remains of once-living things.

▲ Fossils can form by the process of petrification, in which plant and animal parts are changed into stone.

▲ Fossils—in the form of molds, casts, and imprints—record the shapes of living things that have been buried in sediments.

▲ Fossils of entire animals are formed as the animals are buried in tar, amber, or ice.

▲ Trace fossils are any marks formed by an animal and preserved as fossils.

▲ Fossils indicate that many different life forms have existed throughout Earth's history.

1–2 A History in Rocks and Fossils

▲ The law of superposition states that in a series of sedimentary rock layers, younger rocks normally lie on top of older rocks.

▲ Scientists can tell the order in which past events occurred and the relative times of occurrence by studying sedimentary rock layers, index fossils, and unconformities.

▲ Index fossils are used to identify the age of the sedimentary rock layers containing them.

▲ The half-life of a radioactive element is the amount of time it takes for half the atoms in a sample of that element to decay.

▲ Scientists can determine the absolute age of rocks and fossils by using radioactive-dating techniques.

1–3 A Trip Through Geologic Time

▲ Scientists have set up a geologic calendar, divided into four eras: the Precambrian, the Paleozoic, the Mesozoic, and the Cenozoic.

▲ The Precambrian Era began 4.6 billion years ago. During this era, the first plant life formed in the seas.

▲ The Paleozoic Era began 570 million years ago. Sea animals, land plants, and land animals appeared during the Paleozoic Era. Reptiles were the first land animals able to survive out of water.

▲ The Mesozoic Era—containing the Triassic, Jurassic, and Cretaceous periods—began about 225 million years ago. During this time mammals, dinosaurs, and birds evolved.

▲ The Cenozoic Era, which includes the Tertiary and Quaternary periods, began 65 million years ago. During that time the first horses and the first humans evolved.

Reviewing Key Terms

Define each term in a complete sentence.

1–1 Fossils—Clues to the Past

fossil
sediment
petrification
mold
cast
imprint
trace fossil
evolve

1–2 A History in Rocks and Fossils

law of superposition
index fossil
unconformity
fault
intrusion
extrusion
half-life

Chapter Review

Content Review

Multiple Choice

Choose the letter of the answer that best completes each statement.

1. The shape of an organism preserved in rock is called a(an)
   a. mold and cast.   c. imprint.
   b. coprolite.   d. petrification.
2. Bodies of whole animals have been preserved in
   a. ice.   c. amber.
   b. tar.   d. all of these
3. Rocks formed from the piling up of layers of dust, dirt, and sand are called
   a. igneous.   c. magma.
   b. metamorphic.   d. sedimentary.
4. A crack in a rock structure that moves the rocks on either side out of line is a(an)
   a. fault.   c. intrusion.
   b. cast.   d. extrusion.
5. The decay rate of a radioactive element is measured by a unit called
   a. period.   c. half-life.
   b. era.   d. unconformity.
6. Dinosaurs found at Bone Cabin Quarry lived during the
   a. Paleozoic Era.   c. Cretaceous Period.
   b. Jurassic Period. d. Tertiary Period.
7. The animal used as an index fossil for the Paleozoic Era is the
   a. sago palm.   c. trilobite.
   b. dinosaur.   d. *Eryops.*
8. A measure of how many years ago an event occurred or an organism lives is
   a. absolute age. c. decay time.
   b. relative age. d. sedimentary age.

True or False

If the statement is true, write "true." If it is false, change the underlined word or words to make the statement true.

1. The <u>soft</u> parts of plants or animals usually become fossils.
2. An empty space called a <u>cast</u> is left in a rock when a buried organism dissolves.
3. Footprints of extinct dinosaurs are examples of <u>trace fossils</u>.
4. Sediments are usually deposited in <u>vertical</u> layers.
5. The measure of how many years ago an event occurred or an animal lived is called <u>relative age</u>.
6. <u>Faults</u> are always younger than the rock layers they cut through.
7. The time it takes for half the atoms in a sample of a radioactive element to decay is called its <u>half-life</u>.

Concept Mapping

Complete the following concept map for Section 1–1. Refer to pages F6–F7 to construct a concept map for the entire chapter.

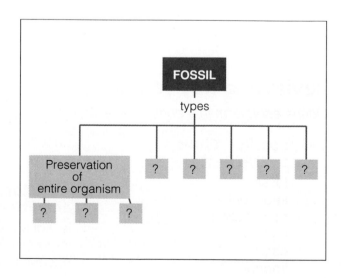

Concept Mastery

Discuss each of the following in a brief paragraph.

1. How are radioactive elements used to determine the age of rocks and fossils?
2. Describe some of the geologic changes that occurred during the Paleozoic Era.
3. Why is sedimentation rate an inaccurate way of measuring geologic time?
4. Why are few fossils found in igneous or metamorphic rock?
5. Discuss five ways fossils can form.
6. Trilobites are important index fossils for the Paleozoic Era. Explain what is meant by this statement.

Critical Thinking and Problem Solving

Use the skills you have developed in this chapter to answer each of the following.

1. **Making calculations** A radioactive element has a half-life of 500 million years. After 2 billion years, how many half-lives have passed? How many kilograms of a 10-kilogram sample would be left at this time? If the half-life were 4 billion years?

2. **Analyzing diagrams** Use the diagram to answer the following questions.
   a. According to the way in which layers C, D, E, and F lie, what might have happened in the past?
   b. Which letter shows an unconformity? Explain your answer.
   c. List the events that occurred from oldest to youngest. Include the order in which each layer was deposited and when the fault, intrusion, and unconformity were formed. Explain why you chose this order.

3. **Interpreting evidence** Suppose you are a scientist who finds some fossils while looking at a cross section of rock in an area. One layer of rock has fossils of the extinct woolly mammoth. In a layer of rock below this, you discover the fossils of an extinct alligator. What can you determine about changes over time in the climate of this area?

4. **Developing a theory** Explain why an animal species that reproduces every year would have a better chance of surviving a change in its environment than an animal species that reproduces only once or twice in ten years does.

5. **Sequencing events** List five events in your life in the order they happened. Have a friend or classmate list five events in his or her life in the order they happened. Now try to list all ten events in the order they happened.

   What difficulties did you have in deciding whether a certain event occurred before or after other events? How has this activity helped you understand the difficulty scientists had in developing a time scale without radioactive dating?

6. **Using the writing process** Choose one of the four geologic eras and write a short story depicting a day in the life of an organism living during that era.

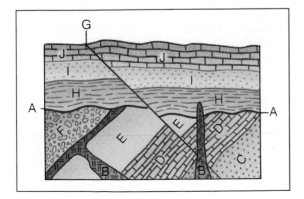

Changes in Living Things Over Time

Guide for Reading

After you read the following sections, you will be able to

2–1 Evolution: Change Over Time
- Describe evidence of evolution.

2–2 Charles Darwin and Natural Selection
- Define and describe natural selection.

2–3 The Development of a New Species
- Describe the processes of speciation and adaptive radiation.

2–4 Punctuated Equilibrium
- Describe punctuated equilibrium and relate it to adaptive radiation.

In the fall of 1991, scientists from Montana State University, the University of Wyoming, and the Royal Tyrell Museum of Canada quickly prepared to leave on an unusual rescue mission. No, they weren't going to rescue an injured camper. Nor were they trying to save an animal in danger. In fact, they were going to rescue a creature that had died about 150 million years ago!

The scientists were on their way to northern Wyoming, where the first intact skeleton of a dinosaur called *Allosaurus* had been discovered. Until then, only bits and pieces of *Allosaurus* bones had been found, but never a complete skeleton. The rescue mission involved preserving the find before the harsh Wyoming winter set in.

Even as you read this chapter, other fossils that provide clues to Earth's past are being sought. The Earth gives up its secrets grudgingly, one clue at a time. Do we have all the answers? Not by a long shot. But we do know a good deal about the changes that have occurred in living things over time—changes we call the evolution of living things.

Journal *Activity*

You and Your World Suppose you were lucky enough to discover the bones of a creature that walked the Earth millions of years ago. In your journal, describe your thoughts and feelings about finding an organism never before seen by people. If you wish, include a drawing of your find.

◀ Allosaurus, *which lived about 140 million years ago, was one of the fiercest predators ever to walk the Earth. It was also one of the largest—about 8 meters long!*

2–1 Evolution: Change Over Time

In Chapter 1 you read about Earth's history. You learned that by studying rocks and fossils, scientists have developed a fairly accurate picture of how Earth and its inhabitants have changed over time. Although the picture is far from complete, there is no doubt that changes have occurred and that many of the living things on Earth today are very different from the living things that existed in the past. In other words, there is no doubt that living things have changed over time.

How and why have living things changed? And which living things are more closely related to one another? Today scientists know that the answers to these questions lie in the process of **evolution.** The word evolution comes from Latin and means an unfolding or opening out. A scientific translation of this meaning is descent with modification. Descent means to come from something that lived before. And modification means change. Thus evolution means that all inhabitants of Earth are changed forms of living things that came before.

Evolution can be defined as a change in species over time. A species is a group of organisms that share similar characteristics and that can interbreed with one another to produce fertile offspring. Lions,

Figure 2–1 *The members of the species* Alces alces, *better known as moose, often wade into lakes and ponds to graze on water plants. What is a species?*

for example, are a species. So are tigers. Lions and tigers share many similar characteristics and can even be bred together to produce offspring called ligers and tiglons. The offspring, however, are not fertile. That is, ligers and tiglons cannot mate and produce more of their own kind. So lions and tigers are not the same species. They are two separate species. Quite the opposite is true of a German shepherd and a French poodle. Although they appear quite different, they can interbreed and produce fertile offspring. So dogs, even though they may appear quite different, are all members of the same species.

Why have some species evolved into the plants and animals living on Earth today while other species became extinct? During the history of life on Earth, chance changes in the genes of organisms have produced new or slightly modified living things. A gene is a unit of heredity that is passed on from parent to offspring. A change in a gene will produce a change in the offspring of an organism. Changes in genes are called mutations. And mutations are one of the driving forces behind evolution.

Mutations: Agents of Change

Most of the time, a mutation in a gene produces an organism that cannot compete with other organisms. This new organism usually dies off quickly. Sometimes, however, the change in the organism is a positive one. The change makes the organism better suited to its environment. A change that increases an organism's chances of survival is called an **adaptation.**

Organisms that are better adapted to their environment do more than just survive. They are able to produce offspring, which produce more offspring, and so on. Over a long period of time, so many small adaptations may occur that a new species may evolve. The new species may no longer resemble its ancient ancestors. In addition, the new species may be so successful in its environment that the species from which it evolved can no longer compete. The original species dies off. Thus the development of a new species can result in the extinction of another species.

ACTIVITY READING

A Packy-Poem

Ever wonder how poets view those "terrible lizards" we call dinosaurs. For a humorous point of view, read the poem *Pachycephalosaurus* by Richard Armour.

Figure 2–2 *A hummingbird's beak, a giraffe's neck, and a vampire bat's sharp teeth are all examples of adaptations for feeding. What are adaptations? How do these particular adaptations affect the animals that have them?*

The Fossil Record

In Chapter 1 you read about the many types of fossils that have been found. The record of Earth's history in fossils and in fossil-containing rocks clearly demonstrates that living things have evolved, or changed over time. You can see some of these changes for yourself in Figure 2–3, which shows the fossil record of the camel. Scientists have cataloged the evolution of many organisms, such as the camel.

The fossil record provides evidence about the changes that have occurred in living things and their way of life. In 1983, for example, scientists found a buried skull belonging to an animal that had lived more than 50 million years ago. The skull was very similar to that of a whale. But the bony structure that allowed the animal to hear could not have worked underwater. So scientists concluded that the whalelike skull belonged to an ancestor of modern whales that spent some of its life on land. Scientists also concluded that at some point the ancestors of whales left the land completely and became water-dwelling creatures.

Although the fossil record is not complete—and never will be because many organisms have come and gone without leaving any fossils—it does provide

Figure 2–3 *Living things have evolved, or changed over time. The diagram shows the fossil record of the past 65 million years in the evolution of the camel. How are modern camels similar to their ancestors? How are they different?*

Labels on skulls (top to bottom): Pleistocene, Pliocene, Miocene, Oligocene, Eocene, Paleocene

ample evidence that evolution has indeed occurred. Fortunately, fossils are but one piece of evidence of evolution. Now let's look into some other ways scientists explore the evolution of living things.

Anatomical Evidence of Change

In the early 1800s, a French biologist named Jean-Baptiste de Lamarck came to the conclusion that living things had changed over time. In his book *Philosophie zoologique,* Lamarck suggested that species seemingly very different could be proven by close study to have developed from the same ancestors. "All forms of life could be organized into one vast family tree," he said. Lamarck's writings were a milestone in biology, as he was one of the first scientists to recognize that evolution had occurred. At the time, Lamarck's theories were contrary to popular beliefs.

Despite his insight into the concept of evolution, Lamarck proved to be wrong about most of his theories concerning the process of evolution. Lamarck believed that organisms change because of an inborn will to change. He believed, for example, that the ancestors of birds had a desire to fly. Over many years, that desire enabled birds to acquire wings—and to be better adapted to their environment as well.

Lamarck also believed that organisms could change their body structure by using body parts in new ways. For example, because birds tried so hard to use their front limbs for flying, the limbs eventually changed into wings. In much the same way, Lamarck reasoned, a body part would eventually grow smaller or even disappear from disuse. For example, by slithering along the ground, a snake would eventually lose its limbs.

As you have read earlier, one of the driving forces behind evolution are mutations. And mutations are changes in genes. Lamarck's beliefs about how and why organisms change are incorrect. Wanting a new body part cannot cause a mutation. Using a body part in a different way—or not using it at all—cannot cause a mutation. Mutations happen; they are chance events. Mutations are independent of a desire to change and of a need to adapt to the environment.

Although Lamarck failed to explain the mechanics of evolution, he did provide a new way of studying living things. All of Lamarck's theories were based on the evidence of anatomy. Anatomy is the study of the physical structure of living things.

Look closely at the structure of the bones in the bat's wing, dog's foreleg, whale's fin, and human's arm in Figure 2–5. Do you see any similarities in the shapes and arrangement of the bones of these animals? You should, because similarities do exist. These similarities indicate that each organism has evolved from a common ancestor. The whale became

Figure 2–4 *Although Lamarck was one of the first scientists to recognize that evolution occurred, his theories about how and why evolution took place proved to be incorrect. How would Lamarck have explained the evolution of the ostrich's strong legs for running? The snake's lack of limbs? How would a modern scientist explain their evolution?*

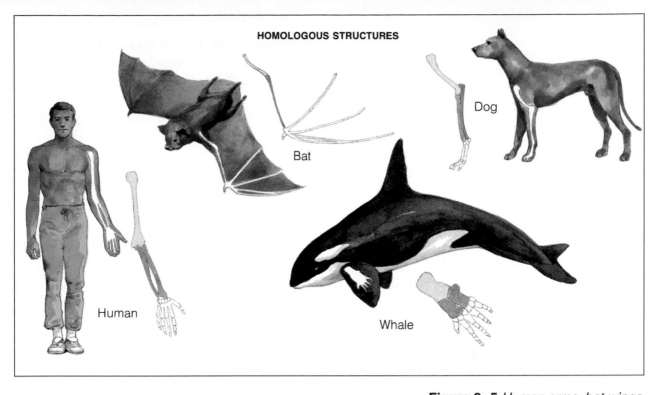

HOMOLOGOUS STRUCTURES

Bat

Dog

Human

Whale

Figure 2–5 *Human arms, bat wings, whale flippers, and dog legs are superbly adapted to performing different tasks. However, their internal structure is remarkably similar. What are such structures called? What do they indicate?*

better adapted to an ocean environment as the structure of its bones gradually changed to those found in the fins of a modern whale. Similarly, the bones of a bat's forelimbs gradually evolved into those found in the wings of modern bats. Structures such as these that evolve from the same ancestral body parts are called **homologous** (hoh-MAH-luh-guhs) **structures.** It was through the study of homologous structures that Lamarck concluded that living things had evolved and had become better adapted to their environment.

Embryological Evidence of Change

By the end of the nineteenth century, scientists had observed that the embryos of many different animals appeared so similar that it was difficult to tell them apart. An embryo is an organism in its early stages of development. Look at Figure 2–6 on page 54. As you can see, the embryos of a fish, chicken, rabbit, and human appear almost identical in their early stages. What does this mean?

The growth and development of an embryo is controlled by its genes. Similarities in the embryos of different organisms indicate that these organisms share a common ancestor. That is, these organisms all share a common heritage. As the embryos

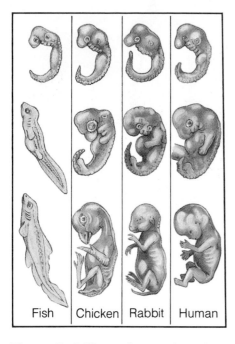

Fish | Chicken | Rabbit | Human

Figure 2–6 *The embryos of vastly different animals look quite similar during the earliest stages of development. These similarities in development hint at genes inherited from a common ancestor.*

continue to develop, other genes take over and the embryo becomes a fish, a chicken, a rabbit, or a human, depending on its gene structure. However, the similarities in the early stages of embryo development are further evidence that living things have evolved from earlier living things and that many living things share a common ancestor.

Chemical Evidence of Change

The quagga vanished from its home in South Africa about 100 years ago. Descriptions of the animal create a strange picture. The quagga had stripes like a zebra. But the stripes covered only its head, neck, and the front part of its body. Was this animal closely related to the zebra? Or was it a completely different kind of creature?

One type of evidence that might show if the zebra and the quagga evolved from a common ancestor is chemical similarities in their DNA. Earlier you read that genes are the units of heredity in living things. Genes are located on chromosomes, which are made of DNA. (The term DNA stands for deoxyribonucleic acid.)

From an evolutionary point of view, the more closely related two living things are, the more similar the structure of their DNA molecules will be. In 1985, Dr. Allen Wilson of the University of California at Berkeley analyzed DNA taken from muscle tissue of a preserved quagga. The tissue of the quagga had

Figure 2–7 *The DNA in a living zebra is 95 percent identical to that of the extinct quagga. This indicates that zebras and quaggas belong to separate but closely related species.*

Figure 2-8 *Seventeen million years ago, a leaf fell from a tree and was perfectly preserved in mud. DNA studies revealed that the plant that dropped the leaf was related to the Chinese magnolia. By comparing DNA from the fossil leaf to DNA from the living plant, scientists can determine how fast DNA changes over time.*

been stored for more than a hundred years in a German museum. Dr. Wilson also analyzed DNA taken from a modern-day zebra. The structure of the DNA in the two samples was 95 percent identical.

Dr. Wilson concluded that the quagga and the zebra were, indeed, close relatives who shared a common ancestor about 3 million years ago. In other words, both the quagga and the zebra evolved from an animal that lived earlier. Scientists use this method of DNA comparison to show the relationships among many other types of organisms as well.

Molecular Evidence of Change

You have just read how similarities in DNA structure can be used to show relationships between organisms. Similarities in other kinds of molecules can be used in an almost identical way. Proteins are molecules that are used to build and repair body parts. Scientists believe that the more similar the structure of protein molecules of different organisms, the more closely related the organisms are. Scientists further believe that the closer the similarity in protein structure of different organisms, the more recently their common ancestor existed.

Scientists have developed a method of measuring the difference between the proteins of different species. In addition, scientists have developed a scale that can be used to estimate the rate of change in proteins over time. This scale of protein change is called a **molecular clock.**

By comparing the similarities in protein structure of different organisms, scientists can determine if the organisms have a common ancestor. If they do,

ACTIVITY
DOING

Extinct Species

Visit a museum of natural history. Find the exhibits of extinct animals such as dinosaurs, woolly mammoths, saber-toothed cats, and others. Find out when and where each of these animals lived. Also find out the reasons scientists believe these animals became extinct. Present your findings to the class.

Figure 2–9 *These strange-looking animals are not purely a product of the artist's imagination. They are based on fossils seven million years old. Like all living things, these animals evolved through modification of earlier life forms.*

the molecular clock can be used to determine how long ago the organisms branched off from that ancestor.

What do all these various types of evidence tell us? From fossils to molecular clocks, the answer is clear. **Living things have evolved through modification of earlier life forms. That is, living things have descended from a common ancestor.**

2–1 Section Review

1. Define evolution, using the term species in your definition.
2. Why are mutations called agents of change?
3. Describe the evidence that supports evolution.

Critical Thinking—*Applying Concepts*
4. Are birds' wings and butterflies' wings homologous structures?

2–2 Charles Darwin and Natural Selection

Guide for Reading

Focus on this question as you read.

▶ *What is natural selection?*

The Galapagos Islands rise out of the Pacific Ocean about 1000 kilometers from the west coast of South America. The islands received their name from the giant Galapagos tortoises that live there. The tortoises' long necks, wrinkled skin, and mud-caked shells make them look like prehistoric creatures. Sharing the islands with the tortoises are many other animals, including penguins, long-necked diving birds called cormorants, and large, crested lizards called iguanas.

The most striking thing about the animals of the Galapagos is the way in which they differ from related species on the mainland of South America. For example, the iguanas on the Galapagos have extra-large claws that allow them to keep their grip on slippery rocks, where they feed on seaweed. On the mainland, iguanas have smaller claws. Smaller claws allow the mainland iguanas to climb trees, where they feed on leaves.

In 1831, a young British student named Charles Darwin set sail for a five-year voyage on a ship called the *Beagle*. Serving as the ship's naturalist, Darwin studied animals and plants at every stop the ship made. When Darwin arrived at the Galapagos, he soon noticed many of the differences between island and mainland creatures. As he compared the animals on the mainland to those on the islands, he realized something special. It appeared that

Figure 2–10 *A giant tortoise from the Galapagos Islands (left) looks quite different from its much smaller cousin from the South American mainland (right). Observations of the tortoises and other creatures of the Galapagos helped to inspire Darwin's theory of evolution.*

Figure 2–11 *A green iguana's long toes, sharp claws, and green scales make it well suited for life in a tropical rain forest (left). Although they evolved from lizards similar to the green iguana, marine iguanas have webbed toes, thick claws, and brownish-gray scales. Their webbed toes and rounded snouts are adaptations for swimming (right).*

Where Are They?, p. 106

each animal was perfectly adapted to survival in its particular environment.

Darwin took many notes and collected many specimens. For the next 20 years he tried to find an underlying theory that could explain his observations. In 1858, Darwin and another British biologist, Alfred Wallace, presented independently a new and exciting concept—the theory of evolution.

This theory was discussed by Darwin in a book entitled *On the Origin of Species*. In this book, Darwin presented an entirely new idea—the concept of **natural selection.** Darwin used this concept to explain how evolution occurs, or the mechanics of evolution. **Natural selection is the survival and reproduction of those organisms best adapted to their surroundings.** To better understand how natural selection works, you must first learn about the role of overproduction in nature.

Overproduction and Natural Selection

Biologists have long known that many species seem to produce more offspring than can be supported by the environment. Every year, for example, dandelions grow seeds with sails that form into a white puff on the stem. The wind blows the seeds through the air. Most seeds land in a place where conditions are unfavorable for new dandelion growth. Only a few seeds land in a place with the right soil, light, and water conditions. These seeds grow into new dandelion plants. Through overproduction, nature assures that at least some seeds will survive to continue the species.

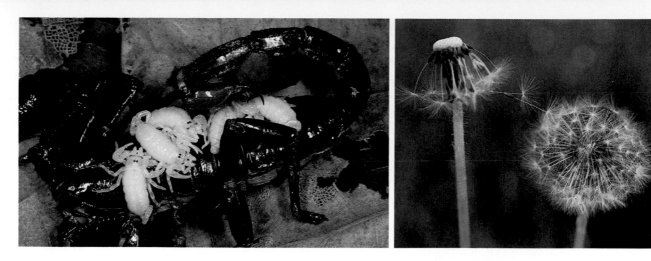

Figure 2–12 *Living things, such as scorpions and dandelions, produce many more offspring than survive. What is the name of the process that determines which individuals survive and reproduce? How does it work?*

Quite often, overproduction of offspring results in competition for food or shelter among the different members of a species. In the case of tadpoles, which hatch from frog eggs, competition can be fierce. The food supply in a pond often is not large enough for every tadpole to survive. Only those strong enough to obtain food and fast enough to avoid enemies will live. These animals will eventually reproduce. The others will die before producing offspring.

The process in which only the best-adapted members of a species survive is sometimes called survival of the fittest. In a sense, the fittest animals are selected, or chosen, by their surroundings to survive. This is basically what Darwin meant by natural selection—nature selects the fittest.

Variation and Natural Selection

Although the members of a species are enough alike to mate, normally no two are exactly the same. In other words, even members of the same species have small variations. For example, some polar bears have thicker coats of fur than others do. This thicker fur gives them more protection against the cold. Such polar bears are fitter, and thus more likely to survive and pass on the characteristic. In this case, a variation in a species will cause some members to survive and reproduce. Over time, the variation will become the norm as those members of the species with the variation survive in greater numbers than do those members without the variation. Can you think of another example of variation in a species?

Activity Bank

Variety Is the Spice of Life, p. 108

ACTIVITY

DISCOVERING

Survival of the Fittest

Scatter a box of red and green toothpicks in a grassy area. Then have a friend pick up in 10 minutes as many toothpicks as he or she can.

Was one color toothpick collected more than the other color? If so, explain why.

■ How can a variation such as color affect the process of natural selection?

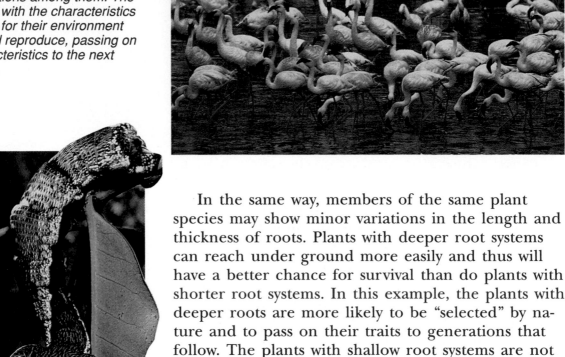

Figure 2–13 *Although these flamingoes may look alike, there are some variations among them. The flamingoes with the characteristics best suited for their environment survive and reproduce, passing on their characteristics to the next generation.*

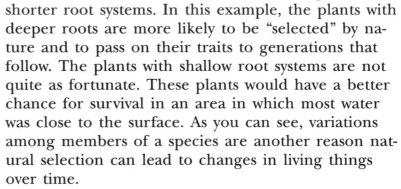

Figure 2–14 *Natural selection may produce some amazing results. The markings and behavior of this caterpillar trick hungry birds into thinking that it is a bird-eating snake. The color and irregular shape of the horned frog make it hard to see among the leaves on the forest floor.*

In the same way, members of the same plant species may show minor variations in the length and thickness of roots. Plants with deeper root systems can reach under ground more easily and thus will have a better chance for survival than do plants with shorter root systems. In this example, the plants with deeper roots are more likely to be "selected" by nature and to pass on their traits to generations that follow. The plants with shallow root systems are not quite as fortunate. These plants would have a better chance for survival in an area in which most water was close to the surface. As you can see, variations among members of a species are another reason natural selection can lead to changes in living things over time.

Minor variations in a species are common. Sometimes, however, mutations can cause a change in an organism's characteristics that is far from minor. For example, in White Sands National Monument in New Mexico, the sand dunes are white. White mice live on these dunes. The light color of the mice is a result of a helpful mutation. Because white mice blend in better with their environment than darker mice do, they are less likely to be eaten by predators. If a mutation occurred that darkened some of the mice, these darker mice would not be able to blend in with their surroundings. The mutation that caused the darker color would be considered a harmful mutation. In this case, natural selection would "weed out" the mice with the harmful mutation. As generations of mice reproduced, the darker mice, along with their harmful mutation, would be eliminated from the species. The white mice with the helpful mutation would survive and multiply.

Mirrors of Change

In some ways living things become a mirror of the changes in their surroundings. The British peppered moth is a recent example of this phenomenon. In the 1850s, most of the peppered moths near Manchester, England, were gray in color. Only a few black moths existed. Because the gray moths were almost the same color as the tree trunks on which they lived, they were nearly invisible to the birds that hunted them for food. Most of the black moths, however, were spotted by the birds and eaten. The species as a whole survived because of the gray moths. Then changes in environmental conditions had a drastic effect on the moths that lived in the area.

As more factories were built in the area, soot from the chimneys blackened the tree trunks. The gray moths could now be seen against the tree trunks. The few surviving black moths, however, now blended in with the tree trunks. As a result, they survived. These moths produced more black offspring. In time, practically all peppered moths were black. Again, the species as a whole survived.

The tale of the peppered moths illustrates how natural selection was able to turn an unusual trait into a common one in a relatively short period of time. As pollution controls in England become tighter in the years to come, how might the peppered moth species be affected?

Figure 2–15 *After the start of the Industrial Revolution, the light gray bark of trees was darkened by the soot from factories. In each photograph, which peppered moth would most likely be noticed by a hungry bird? How did pollution affect the way that natural selection acted upon peppered moths?*

2–2 Section Review

1. Why is natural selection another way of saying survival of the fittest?
2. What is the relationship between overproduction of offspring and natural selection?
3. Describe how living things can become a mirror of the changes in their environment.

Connection—*Ecology*

4. There is evidence that Earth's climate is getting warmer. This phenomenon is called global warming. How might global warming affect the evolution of living things?

2–3 The Development of a New Species

You have seen how, through natural selection, the fittest organisms survive and reproduce. Natural selection explains how variations in a species can lead to changes in that species. But how does an entirely new species evolve? Recall that a species is a group of organisms that share similar characteristics and that can interbreed and produce fertile offspring. In order to understand how a new species forms, you have to know a bit more about competition among organisms.

Niche

Every type of living thing has certain needs that must be filled in order for that living thing to survive. For example, organisms need food, shelter, and water. The combination of an organism's needs (which must be supplied by the environment), its habitat (where it lives), and the role it plays in its habitat (how it affects and is affected by the living and nonliving things around it) is called the organism's **niche.** A lion's niche, for example, is found in the plains of Africa. A lion would not survive outside its niche—for example, in the cold arctic climate. A polar bear's niche, on the other hand, is found in the cold arctic. A polar bear would not survive on the African plains.

Figure 2–16 *An organism's niche includes everything an organism does and everything an organism needs in its environment. Can you explain why lions would not be able to occupy the same niche as zebras or polar bears? What might happen if catlike meat-eaters that lived in grasslands and hunted large animals were introduced into the lions' environment?*

One general rule of biology is that when two organisms occupy the same niche, they strongly compete with each other for food, shelter, and water. If two organisms occupy different niches, they do not strongly compete with each other. If two species of birds, for example, live in the same tree, but one species lives in the upper branches and feeds on insects found on those branches and the other species lives on the lower branches and feeds on different insects on those branches, then the two species occupy different niches. They live in the same tree, but they are not in competition for the same niche. As you continue to read about niches, keep in mind that a niche can be very small and specific.

When two species occupy the same niche, one species will be successful and survive and the other species will be less successful and possibly become extinct. When two species occupy different niches, they both have a better chance for survival. **In general, new species evolve when there are empty niches that can be filled or when a species moves into a niche it did not previously occupy.**

Migration and Isolation

There are two common ways in which organisms may move into a new or empty niche. One way is through migration. In simple terms, migration means moving from the place in which an organism lives to a new home. During Earth's long history, many organisms have migrated to new areas. Once in a new area, the organism may move into a new niche. If the niche is empty, there will be no competition. If the niche is not empty, competition will arise. Either the new organism or the organism that originally lived in that niche will die off.

The other way an organism may occupy a new niche is through isolation. Isolation occurs when some members of a species suddenly become cut off from the rest of that species. Isolation may be due to barriers that form over time. For example, when a mountain range rises, the organisms living on each side of the range become isolated from one another. (Sure that takes a long time, but evolution can be a very long process.) As the members of a species become isolated from one another, they may begin

ACTIVITY
WRITING

Warmblooded Dinosaurs?

For many years, scientists believed that dinosaurs were coldblooded, as are modern reptiles. Now, however, there is much evidence that at least some dinosaur species were warmblooded. Using reference materials, write a report on warmblooded dinosaurs, providing evidence for and against the theory. At the end of your report, give your opinion. You must back up your opinion with solid scientific evidence.

Figure 2–17 *In Australia, pouched mammals evolved to fill niches that are occupied by other types of mammals elsewhere in the world. The kangaroo, surprisingly, is the Australian equivalent of an antelope—a large, fast-moving plant-eater that lives in large groups. The cat-sized cuscus lives in trees, eats fruit and small animals, has a grasping tail, and is quite curious. What familiar animal occupies a niche similar to that of the cuscus?*

to fill different niches, particularly if the geography and climate in the area change as well.

In Chapter 1 you read about a very dramatic example of isolation. Hundreds of millions of years ago, all of Earth's landmasses were combined in the supercontinent called Pangaea. Over time, Pangaea split into the continents that exist on Earth today. As the continents separated, species became isolated from one another and began to occupy new niches. Perhaps the most striking illustration of this process of isolation is the continent of Australia. The organisms living in Australia have been isolated from all other organisms on Earth for millions of years. As a consequence, organisms in Australia have evolved in different ways from organisms in the rest of the world. And that is why many of the living things in Australia are so different from living things found almost everywhere else on Earth.

Speciation: Occupying New Niches

Scientists use the term speciation to describe the development of a new species. Perhaps the best way to explain how migration, empty niches, and isolation can lead to the evolution of a new species is through an example. Imagine that a species of birds lives in a particular area. All the birds eat the tiny seeds of a shrub that grows in that area. Now imagine that through barriers or perhaps through the movement of continents, the birds become separated into three different areas. In the first area, the shrubs with the seeds the birds eat still thrive. In the second area, the shrubs are no longer common. Instead, different shrubs with larger seeds grow. In the third area, very few seed-bearing shrubs exist. But shrubs with berries grow extremely well.

Now assume that before the isolation, the beaks of the birds were well adapted to picking up and breaking open the small seeds of the shrubs. The birds that have been isolated in the area with the same shrubs still occupy the same niche. Thus they will probably not change much over time. They will be successful by staying in the niche they occupy.

As you have just read, the shrubs in the second area have larger seeds. The birds there have a difficult time picking up and breaking open the seeds. However, one day a mutation or variation in the birds produces a bird with a larger, stronger beak. This bird will be more successful at eating the larger seeds. Over time, the birds with the small beaks will die off as nature selects the fittest birds for survival. Only those birds with the larger, stronger beaks will survive and reproduce.

In the third area, a mutation or variation produces an offspring with a beak well adapted to picking and eating berries. Again, the birds with the small beaks will die off as nature selects the birds with the better adapted beaks—the fitter birds. What do you think might happen to birds born with this adaptation who live in the first area where the shrubs with tiny seeds still grow?

As you can see, over time the beaks of the birds will have changed. The birds in each area will be better adapted to their environment because of the

Figure 2–18 *Natural selection is the most important force behind evolution. However, some changes may occur simply by chance. Natural selection provides an advantage to rhinoceroses with horns. But the African rhinoceros (top) is not more fit than the Indian rhinoceros (bottom) because it has two horns rather than one. During the course of evolution, the two types of rhinoceroses developed different numbers of horns purely by chance.*

changes in the beaks. Furthermore, although this example has concentrated on changes in beaks, you can probably assume that other structural changes will also have occurred as each bird species became better adapted to its environment. Over time, the birds will have changed so much that they can no longer interbreed and produce fertile offspring. In

Figure 2–19 *Adaptive radiation is the process by which many different species develop from a common ancestor. As you can see, some of the descendants of the* cotylosaur *do not resemble it at all!*

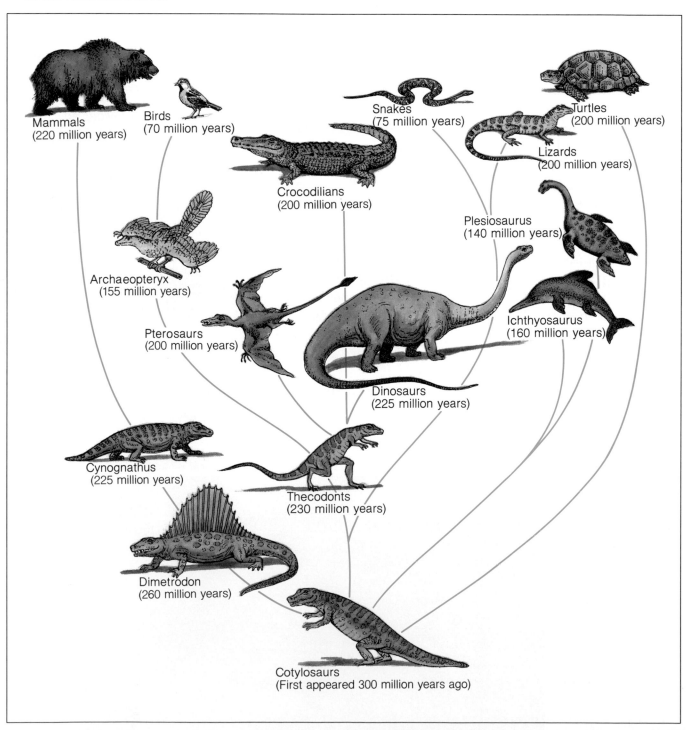

Mammals
(220 million years)

Birds
(70 million years)

Snakes
(75 million years)

Turtles
(200 million years)

Crocodilians
(200 million years)

Lizards
(200 million years)

Plesiosaurus
(140 million years)

Archaeopteryx
(155 million years)

Pterosaurs
(200 million years)

Ichthyosaurus
(160 million years)

Dinosaurs
(225 million years)

Cynognathus
(225 million years)

Thecodonts
(230 million years)

Dimetrodon
(260 million years)

Cotylosaurs
(First appeared 300 million years ago)

other words, several new species of birds will have evolved from the original species.

Although this example has been imaginary, it is quite similar to the situation Darwin encountered in the Galapagos. On the islands of the Galapagos, Darwin found many species of a type of bird called a finch. On each island, the finches were slightly different and had formed a new species. Darwin's finches—just as the birds in our example—had evolved, and those better adapted to each island had survived.

Speciation and Adaptive Radiation

The process in which one species evolves into several species, each of which fills a different niche, is called adaptive radiation. In **adaptive radiation**, organisms of a species "radiate," or move away from, other organisms in that species and occupy new niches. Over time, these organisms may evolve into entirely new species. Keep in mind that in adaptive radiation, the new species all share a common ancestor. You might say they adapted to their new environment as they radiated away from the area where their common ancestor lived. The homologous structures you have read about earlier are evidence of such adaptive radiation in which similar body parts of related organisms evolved to perform different functions.

Living Dinosaurs?

Many biologists assert that the dinosaurs are not extinct, but rather are alive and well. These biologists think that birds are actually modern-day dinosaurs.

Current theory indicates that birds evolved from the most famous of the dinosaurs, *Tyrannosaurus rex.* Using reference materials, find out why birds may be related to *Tyrannosaurus rex.* (*Hint:* You will concentrate on jawbones.)

On posterboard, illustrate those similarities and differences you have discovered between dinosaurs and modern birds.

2–3 Section Review

1. What happens when two species occupy the same niche?
2. What is the relationship between migration, isolation, and speciation?
3. Define adaptive radiation. Use the term niche in your definition.

Connection—*Ecology*

4. As people have moved from place to place, they have often brought plants and animals with them. How might the introduction of a new species of plant or animal in an area have disastrous effects on the organisms already living in that area?

PROBLEM Solving

Darwin's Finches

While in the Galapagos Islands, Charles Darwin conducted detailed studies of the finches that lived there. The illustration below shows the possible evolution of some of the finch species that Darwin studied. The scientific name and beak outline are shown for each species.

Interpreting Evidence

1. How many species of ground finches are present in the Galapagos Islands?
2. What is the primary difference between the main types of finches?
3. Each species has a common name as well as a scientific name. What is the scientific name for the vegetarian tree finch?
4. Which ground finches are cactus-eating finches?
5. Suggest a reason why the sharp beak of the *G. difficilis* differs from the beaks of other ground finches.
6. How does the chart demonstrate evolution?

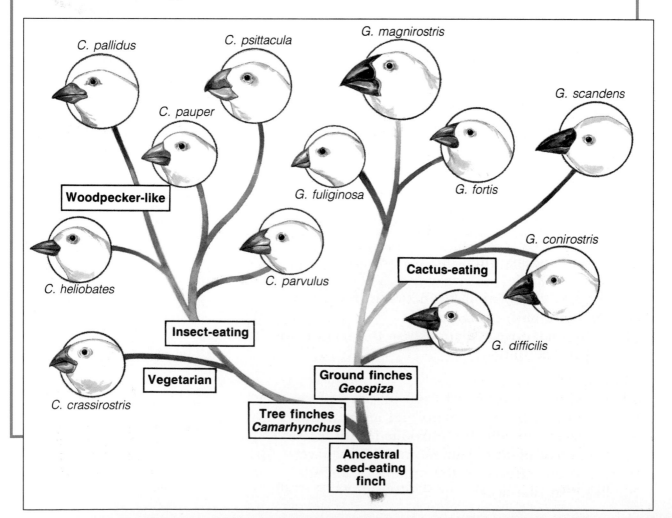

2–4 Punctuated Equilibrium

In Chapter 1 you read about the dinosaurs. Dinosaurs dominated the Earth for more than 150 million years. Then, about 65 million years ago, all living species of dinosaurs became extinct. (Around the same time, about 95 percent of all other living things also became extinct.) Scientists call such extinctions mass extinctions.

Mass extinctions seem rather harsh. After all, suddenly a great many species disappear, never to be seen again. In evolutionary terms, however, mass extinctions play an important role in the development of new species. After a mass extinction, a wide variety of previously occupied niches become available to those species that still exist. And as you might expect, many adaptive radiations occur after a mass extinction, as species move into new niches. In fact, after the mass extinction of the dinosaurs, a type of living thing that had existed for more than 50 million years in the shadow of the dinosaurs underwent a great adaptive radiation. This type of living thing began to fill unoccupied niches throughout the world. Do you know what this type of living thing is? You are correct if you said mammal. You are a mammal. So is a dog, a lion, a whale, and a skunk. Mammals are the dominant life form on Earth today primarily because the dinosaurs died off, leaving so many niches for mammals to fill.

In most cases, natural selection as described by Darwin is a long, slow process. Scientists do not doubt that natural selection occurs or that it leads to the evolution of living things. However, the fossil record shows very little evidence of gradual change. (Remember, most organisms do not leave fossils. So this lack of fossil evidence is to be expected.) But the fossil record does seem to indicate that some species may not change at all for long periods of time. This period of stability, or equilibrium, may continue for millions of years. Then suddenly, a great adaptive radiation may occur and a species may evolve into many new species, filling new niches. The equilibrium is broken, or punctuated.

In 1972, scientists Stephen Jay Gould and Niles Eldridge developed a theory called **punctuated equilibrium.** As you read its definition, keep in mind

Guide for Reading

Focus on this question as you read.

▶ *What is punctuated equilibrium?*

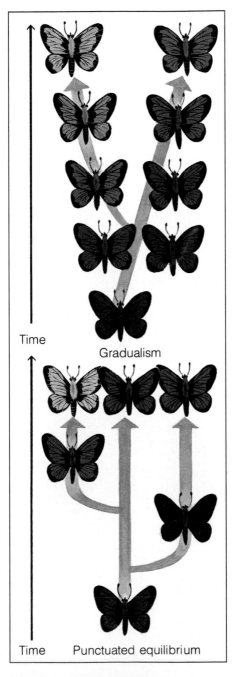

Time

Gradualism

Time   Punctuated equilibrium

Figure 2–20 *Organisms may change slowly and gradually over time. Or they may remain the same for a long time, then change quickly and abruptly.*

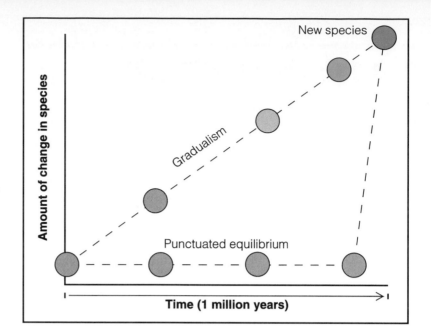

Figure 2–21 *Darwin thought that evolutionary change always occurs slowly and continually. This traditional view of the rate of evolution was challenged by the theory of punctuated equilibrium. In some cases, according to this theory, evolution may be at a standstill most of the time. These long periods of stability are occasionally interrupted by bursts of rapid change.*

Figure 2–22 *Natural disasters such as forest fires create new niches and may open up old ones. How have large-scale natural disasters shaped the evolution of life on Earth?*

that in evolutionary terms, "short" can mean thousands of years. **According to punctuated equilibrium, there may be periods in Earth's history in which many adaptive radiations occur in a relatively short period of time.**

When does punctuated equilibrium seem to occur? As you might expect, it is most common when many niches are opened. This occurs during a mass extinction. It can also occur as a result of isolation, such as the isolation of organisms in Australia.

Today scientists believe that evolution can occur gradually—as described by Darwin—as well as fairly rapidly—as described by Gould and Eldridge. Neither theory disputes the other, and both seem to be valid. That is, punctuated equilibrium does not mean gradual change is incorrect. And Darwin's theory of gradual change does not mean that punctuated equilibrium is incorrect. Both forms of evolution seem to have occurred during Earth's 4.6-billion-year history.

2–4 Section Review

1. What is punctuated equilibrium? What is a mass extinction? How are they related?

Critical Thinking—*Making Inferences*
2. In what ways does the fossil record support punctuated equilibrium?

Planetary Evolution

While we tend to think of evolution as a biological event, the term is relevant to other sciences as well. Astronomers, for example, talk of the evolution of our solar system. The current theory on the evolution of our solar system is called the *nebular theory.*

According to the nebular theory, our solar system evolved from a huge cloud of dust and gas called a nebula. Shock waves, probably from the explosion of a nearby star, disrupted the dust and gas in the nebula. In reaction to the shock waves, the gases in the nebula began to contract inward, causing the nebula to shrink. As it shrank, the dust and gases began to spin around the center of the nebula. In time, the spinning nebula flattened into a huge disk almost 10 billion kilometers in diameter.

Near the center of the disk a new sun or *protosun* began to form. Gases and other matter surrounding the newly formed sun continued to spin. Some of the gas and matter began to clump together. Small clumps became larger and larger clumps. The largest clumps became *protoplanets,* or the beginnings of planets.

Over time the protoplanets near the sun became so hot that most of their gases boiled away, leaving behind a rocky core. Today these planets are known as Mercury, Venus, Earth, and Mars. Planets farther from the sun did not lose their gases because they did not receive as much heat. These planets became the gas giants. Today these gas giants are known as Jupiter, Saturn, Uranus, and Neptune.

Now here's a question for you to try to answer: How do you think Pluto, the ninth planet, formed? *Hint:* Pluto is a cold, barren world much different from the outer gas giants.

Laboratory Investigation

Analyzing a Geologic Time Line

Problem

How can the relationships between evolutionary events be plotted on a time line?

Materials *(per student)*

meterstick
pencil
5 meters of adding-machine tape

Procedure

1. For your time line, use a scale in which 1 mm = 1 million years, or 1 m = 1 billion years.

2. Using the meterstick, draw a continuous straight line down the middle of the tape. Draw a straight line across one end. Label this line *The Present*. Assuming each meter represents 1 billion years, place a label at the spot representing 4.6 billion years ago. Add the label *Earth's Beginning?* to this line.

3. Using the table provided, plot each event on the time-line tape. Label both the number of years ago and the event.

Observations

1. Which time period is the longest? The shortest?

2. In which era did dinosaurs exist or begin to exist? In which era did mammals exist or begin to exist?

3. Which lived on Earth the longer time, dinosaurs or mammals?

Analysis and Conclusions

1. How many years does 1 cm represent on your time scale?

2. Why is there a question mark in the label Earth's Beginning?

3. If you had any difficulty plotting some of the events on the list, explain why.

4. What general conclusions can you draw from your time line regarding gradual evolution versus punctuated equilibrium?

5. **On Your Own** Add any events to your time line that you feel are significant. Use the information you have read in both Chapters 1 and 2.

INFERRED AGES OF EVENTS IN YEARS BEFORE PRESENT	
Event Label	**Number of Years Ago**
First mammals and dinosaurs	200 million
Beginning of Carboniferous Period	345 million
Oldest fungi	1.7 billion
Beginning of Jurassic Period	190 million
Beginning of Devonian Period	395 million
Last ice age	10,000
Beginning of Cretaceous Period	136 million
Beginning of Paleozoic Era (first abundant fossils)	570 million
Oldest rocks known	3.5 billion
Beginning of Quaternary Period	1.8 million
Oldest carbon from plants	3.6 billion
Beginning of Ordovician Period	500 million
First birds	160 million
Beginning of Cenozoic Era	65 million
First humanlike creatures	2–4 million
Beginning of Silurian Period	430 million
First reptiles	290 million
Beginning of Mesozoic Era	225 million
Modern humans make tools	500,000
Beginning of Permian Period	280 million

Study Guide

Summarizing Key Concepts

2–1 Evolution: Change Over Time

▲ Evolution can be defined as a change in species over time.

▲ A species is a group of organisms that share similar characteristics and can interbreed to produce fertile offspring.

▲ Scientists use fossil evidence, anatomical evidence, embryological evidence, chemical evidence, and molecular evidence to demonstrate that evolution has occurred during Earth's 4.6-billion-year history.

▲ By studying homologous structures, Lamarck demonstrated that living things may share common ancestors. Homologous structures are structures that have evolved from the same body parts.

2–2 Charles Darwin and Natural Selection

▲ Based on his observations of organisms in the Galapagos, Charles Darwin developed a theory of evolution that described evolutionary changes as a result of natural selection.

▲ Natural selection is the survival and reproduction of those organisms best adapted to their surroundings.

2–3 The Development of a New Species

▲ In general, organisms that share the same niche must compete with one another. Organisms that occupy separate niches do not compete.

▲ New species evolve when there are empty niches that can be filled or when a species moves into a niche it did not previously occupy.

▲ Speciation, or the development of a new species, may occur when an organism becomes adapted to a new niche.

▲ The process by which one species evolves into several species, each of which fills a different niche, is called adaptive radiation.

2–4 Punctuated Equilibrium

▲ According to the punctuated equilibrium theory, there may be periods in Earth's history in which many adaptive radiations occur in a relatively short period of time. Many of these great adaptive radiations occurred after a mass extinction in which many niches were left unoccupied.

Reviewing Key Terms

Define each term in a complete sentence.

2–1 Evolution: Change Over Time
evolution
adaptation
homologous structure
molecular clock

2–2 Charles Darwin and Natural Selection
natural selection

2–3 The Development of a New Species
niche
adaptive radiation

2–4 Punctuated Equilibrium
punctuated equilibrium

Chapter Review

Content Review

Multiple Choice

Choose the letter of the answer that best completes each statement.

1. A term that can be described as descent with modification is
   a. natural selection.
   b. evolution.
   c. isolation.
   d. migration.
2. Which of these is not used as evidence of evolution?
   a. fossils
   b. embryology
   c. niche
   d. homologous structures
3. A bat's wing and a lion's leg bones are examples of
   a. variation.
   b. homologous structures.
   c. migratory effects.
   d. fossils.
4. A change that increases an organism's chances for survival is called a(n)
   a. mutation.
   b. adaptation.
   c. radiation.
   d. homologous structure.
5. Another way to say survival of the fittest is
   a. natural selection.
   b. overproduction.
   c. adaptive radiation.
   d. mutation.
6. The process in which one species evolves into several species is called
   a. mutation.
   b. adaptive radiation.
   c. isolation.
   d. punctuated equilibrium.

True or False

If the statement is true, write "true." If it is false, change the underlined word or words to make the statement true.

1. <u>Natural selection</u> can be defined as descent with modification.
2. Most species produce <u>fewer</u> young than the environment can support.
3. Most members of a species show <u>variation</u>.
4. Evolution can be defined as a change in <u>an organism</u> over time.
5. <u>Migration</u> and <u>isolation</u> are two common ways an organism may move into a new or empty niche.
6. The unusual organisms living in Australia are due to <u>migration</u>.
7. Homologous structures are evidence of <u>adaptive radiation</u>.

Concept Mapping

Complete the following concept map for Section 2–1. Refer to pages F6–F7 to construct a concept map for the entire chapter.

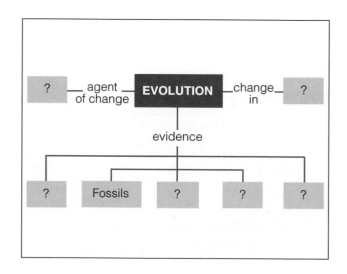

Concept Mastery

Discuss each of the following in a brief paragraph.

1. What does the phrase common descent mean?
2. Discuss the role of overproduction in nature.
3. Use an example to explain the concept of natural selection.
4. Compare migration and isolation.
5. Evolution is an ongoing process. It continues as it has for millions of years. Why are scientists usually unable to see evolution in action?
6. Compare natural selection as described by Darwin and punctuated equilibrium as described by Gould and Eldridge.

Critical Thinking and Problem Solving

Use the skills you have developed in this chapter to answer each of the following.

1. **Making comparisons** Would you expect there to be more similarities between the DNA of a cat and a lion or a cat and a dog? Explain.
2. **Relating cause and effect** Certain snails that live in woods and in grasses are eaten by birds. The snails that live in grasses are yellow. The snails that live on the woodland floor are dark colored. Explain how the snails have become adapted to their environments through natural selection.
3. **Making observations** Observe an animal in your classroom, your home, or a pet store. List five characteristics of the animal, such as hair color or size. Then list possible variations for each characteristic. Finally, explain how each variation might make an animal more fit for survival in its natural environment.
4. **Making inferences** Darwin was amazed at the diversity of life he observed on the Galapagos. How might this diversity have contributed to his ideas regarding evolution?
5. **Evaluating options** Is protecting an endangered species defying natural selection? Explain your answer.
6. **Applying concepts** The giant panda occupies a very small niche by eating only one kind of food: bamboo. How can being adapted to such a small niche actually endanger this species?

7. **Using the writing process** You are a young reporter for a local newspaper near the home of Charles Darwin. You have been asked to interview Darwin about his theory of evolution. Develop a list of five questions you would like to have Darwin discuss. Then see whether you can answer them in the manner Darwin would.

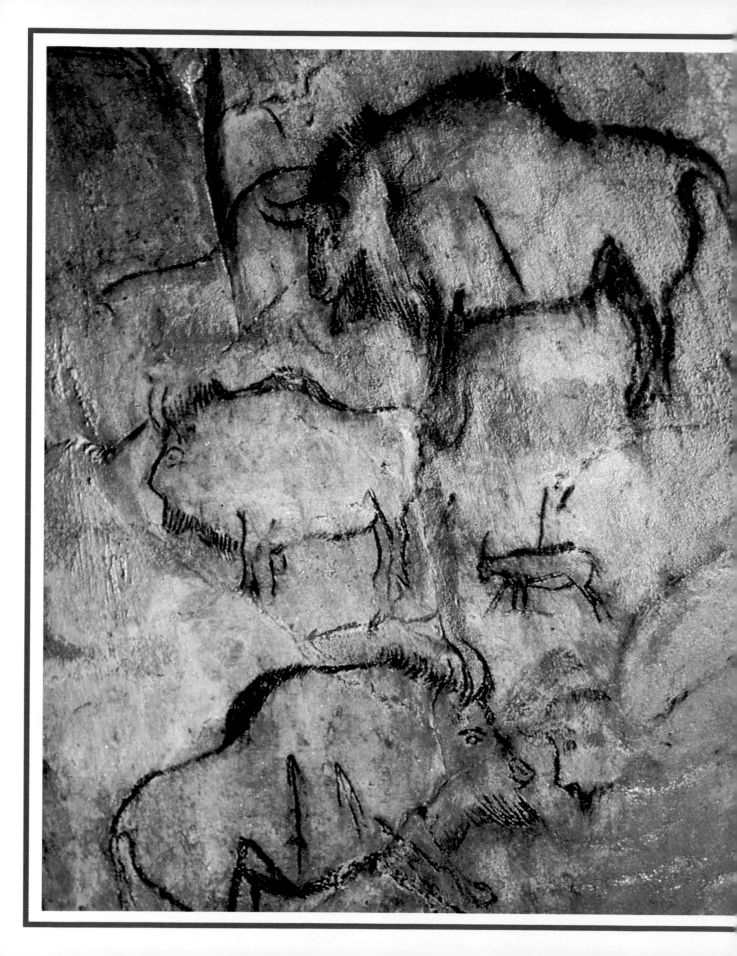

The Path to *Modern Humans*

Guide for Reading

After you read the following sections, you will be able to

3–1 The Search for Human Ancestors

- Describe the characteristics of primates.
- Compare New World monkeys to Old World monkeys.

3–2 Human Ancestors and Relatives

- Describe some early human ancestors.
- Compare Neanderthals and Cro-Magnons.

In 1879, on a farm in northern Spain, a twelve-year-old girl named Maria accidentally made the first discovery of prehistoric art. While exploring a cave with her father, she discovered some remarkable drawings. These drawings pictured deer, wolves, and large bull-like animals. In addition, Maria and her father found stone tools and animal bones—objects that were depicted in the paintings.

Unfortunately, the archaeologists who were told of the discovery dismissed it as a fraud. You see, most archaeologists of the 1800s believed that ancient people had neither the ability nor the intelligence to create such works of art.

Archaeologists today believe that the animals in the cave were painted by skilled artists who lived about 15,000 years ago. Caves with similar paintings have also been found in other parts of Europe. In this chapter you will learn how scientists have used these discoveries to piece together the story of human history. And perhaps one day you will be as lucky as Maria and discover something equally exciting!

Journal *Activity*

You and Your World Focus on your state and predict what the environment will be like in 10,000 years. In your journal, describe the climate, geographic features, composition of the air, type of vegetation, and available natural resources. Make a drawing of your new environment and include a few animals of your own design.

These paintings of bison in a cave in France are similar to those discovered in Spain in 1879.

3–1 The Search for Human Ancestors

The search for the first ancestors of humans is on. All over the Earth, scientists are piecing together details that will shed more light on the exciting study of our past. Anthropologists and archaeologists examine ancient human tools and cultures for answers. Paleontologists study the fossils of ancient humans and compare them with living forms. Biologists examine the DNA (basic substance of heredity) of different species, looking for similarities and differences that determine whether the species are closely related.

Each new fossil find and each new research paper brings a new storm of controversy. Just when scientists think that years of study and debate have brought them a step closer to human origins, a new fossil or a new theory turns up. Then a fresh shadow of doubt is cast on our knowledge of how humans evolved.

There is no doubt among scientists, however, that humans evolved from common ancestors they share with other living primates. Scientists also know that the human species evolved in Africa and then spread around the Earth.

What Are Primates?

Primates are members of a group of mammals that include humans, monkeys, and about 200 other species of living things. **Primates share several important characteristics. All primates have flexible fingers. (Some have flexible toes, too.) Most primates have opposable thumbs.** An opposable thumb is opposite the other fingers and is able to move toward them and touch them. Opposable thumbs enable primates to grasp objects, both large and small.

Generally, primates have much flatter faces than other groups of mammals. Their eyes are located at the front of their heads rather than at the sides, and their snouts are very much reduced in size. As a result of these features, the brains of primates can

Figure 3–1 *Archaeologists are scientists who study the remains of ancient people. These archaeologists are examining some specimens at a site in Chichen-Itza, Mexico.*

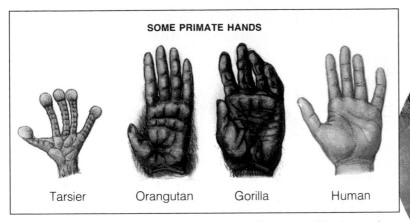

SOME PRIMATE HANDS

Tarsier   Orangutan   Gorilla   Human

Figure 3–2 *Flexible primate fingers and toes enable the red-bellied lemur to sit comfortably in a tree. The hand of the rhesus monkey, which is shown on top of a human hand, has shortened fingers. How are the hands of the tarsier, orangutan, and gorilla similar to the human hand? How are they different?*

combine the separate image from each eye into a single, three-dimensional picture. **The ability to form a three-dimensional picture is another characteristic of primates.** Thus, primates can sense depth and can judge distances. This adaptation is especially helpful when a primate has to locate branches as it swings from one tree to the next.

Primates also have a large and complex cerebrum. The cerebrum is the part of the brain responsible for all the voluntary actions of the body. The behavior of primates is therefore more involved than that of any other animal. For example, primate mothers take care of their young for a longer period of time than most other mammals do. Many species of primates also have complicated social behaviors that include friendships and—sadly—fighting among competing groups.

A New Kind of Primate

On the evolutionary time scale, primates are considered newcomers. Animals have inhabited Earth for more than 600 million years. Mammals have been here for at least 200 million years. In contrast, the first known primates appeared about 70 million years ago—relatively recently.

Some 50 million years ago, the early primates split into two main evolutionary groups—prosimians (proh-SIHM-ee-ehnz) and anthropoids (AN-thruh-poidz). Modern prosimians are almost all nocturnal animals with large eyes adapted for seeing in the

Figure 3–3 *What primate characteristic is shown in this photograph of a tamarin?*

ACTIVITY

DISCOVERING

A Modern Culture

Prepare a display that contains some objects that represent the culture in which you live. Choose objects that would help a scientist 10,000 years from now understand your culture.

■ Explain why you chose the objects you did.

dark. Some examples of living prosimians are lemurs, lorises, and ayes-ayes. Anthropoids are humanlike primates that include monkeys, apes, and humans.

A few million years after the split of prosimians and anthropoids, two anthropoid branches evolved. These branches, the two major groups of monkeys and apes, developed when the continents separated from one another. One group of anthropoids evolved into the monkeys found today in Central and South America. This group is called the New World monkeys. (The term New World comes from the days of Columbus, when the Americas were referred to as the New World.) All New World monkeys live in trees. Many of them have grasping tails, which help them to move through their habitat. New World monkeys include marmosets, howler monkeys, and spider monkeys.

The other group of anthropoids evolved into Old World monkeys and hominoids (HAHM-eh-noidz). Old

Figure 3–4 *This evolutionary tree illustrates how primates may have evolved from early prosimians. Which primates are hominoids?*

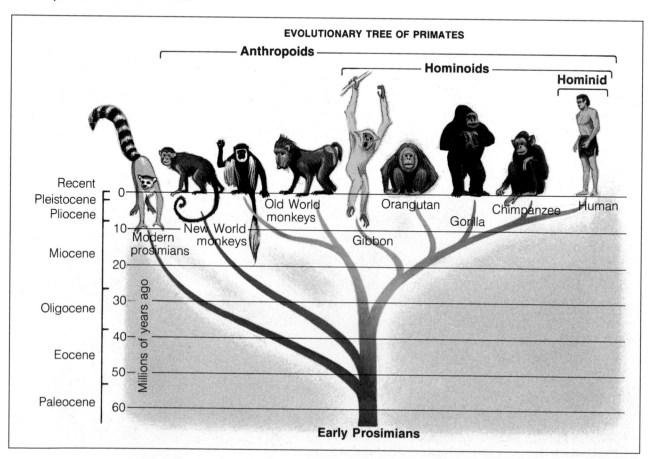

Figure 3–5 *The loris is an example of a modern prosimian (top left). Modern prosimians, almost all of which are nocturnal, are tree-dwelling primates. New World monkeys are also tree-dwelling animals. Some, such as squirrel monkeys (bottom left), can hang from their tails. The macaque is an Old World monkey (right). Old World monkeys do not have grasping tails. They walk on the ground, using all four limbs.*

World monkeys live in Africa and Asia. They do not have grasping tails. Some live in trees; others spend a greater amount of time on the ground. Examples of Old World monkeys are langurs (luhn-GOORZ), baboons, macaques (muh-KAHKS), and rhesus (REE-suhs) monkeys. Hominoids, which are cousins of the Old World monkeys, include apes—gorillas, gibbons, orangutans, chimpanzees—and humans.

3–1 Section Review

1. What are some characteristics of primates?
2. What is three-dimensional vision?
3. How did primates evolve?
4. How are New World monkeys and Old World monkeys the same? How are they different?

Connection—*You and Your World*

5. Design an experiment to demonstrate the advantage of having opposable thumbs.

3–2 Human Ancestors and Relatives

About 6 million years ago, the hominoids gave rise to a small group of species now considered to be the closest relatives to humans. The small group of species is called hominids (HAHM-uh-nihdz). Hominids, which include humans and closely related primates, are members of the human family known as Hominidae (hahm-uh-NIHD-igh). Although these early hominids were not yet humans, they did take evolutionary paths that distinguished them from the other hominoids.

The early hominids experienced changes in the shapes of their spinal column and their hip and leg bones. These changes enabled hominids to walk upright on two legs. In this position the hands of hominids were free to use tools more often. At the same time, the opposable thumb evolved, allowing hominids to grasp objects and use them as tools more effectively than other primates did. In addition, hominids showed an unusual increase in brain size. Even for primates, the brains of hominids were exceptionally large.

Figure 3–6 *Compare the skeleton of a human with the skeleton of an ape. Note the shape of the jaws, the structure of the pelvis, and the way the spine enters the skull.*

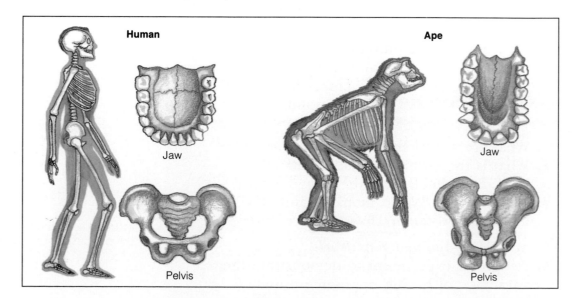

Human	Ape
Jaw	Jaw
Pelvis	Pelvis

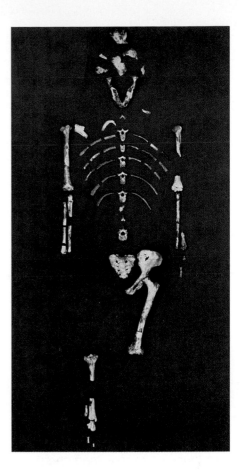

Figure 3–7 *This skeleton of* Australopithecus afarensis *was nicknamed Lucy by its discoverers. Lucy is one of the oldest and most complete of the early hominids yet to be found.*

The First Humanlike Ancestors: *Australopithecus*

In order to determine the course of human evolution, fossils of human ancestors were needed. Much of the evidence for the evolution of hominids came from a small area in eastern Africa between Ethiopia and Tanzania. There, many fossil discoveries of hominids were made.

In 1924, the first fossil of a hominid was discovered in South Africa by the Australian physician Raymond Dart. He named his find *Australopithecus* (Aw-struh-loh-pihth-eh-cuhs), which means southern ape. Because the fossil was that of a child hominid, it was of little help to researchers who needed to know what an adult looked like. Fortunately, a few years later in Africa, researchers did find a fossil of an adult hominid. They named it *Australopithecus africanus* (af-rih-KAHN-uhs). *A. africanus* was hailed as the first human ancestor. (The letter *A.* is an abbreviation for the genus *Australopithecus*.) Most fossil specimens of *A. africanus* are only 2 to 3 million years old. The fossils show a blending of apelike and humanlike characteristics that include small teeth, signs of upright posture, and a brain whose size lies somewhere between that of apes and humans.

In 1974, another more complete hominid fossil was discovered in Ethiopia by a team of researchers led by the American scientists Donald Johanson and Tim White. This humanlike fossil was named *Australopithecus afarensis* (af-uh-REHN-zihs), and nicknamed Lucy. The nickname comes from the Beatles' song "Lucy in the Sky With Diamonds," which was playing on the tape deck at the researchers' camp site. The age of this fossil is estimated at about 3.5 million years. Some scientists immediately proclaimed Lucy to be the earliest human ancestor. Other scientists, however, disagreed.

Whether Lucy is one of the earliest human ancestors is still open to question. From other bones found with Lucy, some scientists have concluded that she walked upright on two legs. Others say that her

Figure 3–8 *These specimens of* Australopithecus africanus, *found in Taung, South Africa, are about 2.5 million years old.*

Figure 3–9 *These 3.6-million-year-old footprints, which were fossilized in volcanic ash, are being unearthed by archaeologists in Laetoli, Tanzania. The trail on the left was made by three hominids. The prints on the right are those of a three-toed horse. What do the footprints tell you about these hominids?*

hands indicate she was adapted to life mainly in the trees. Tree life, of course, would disqualify her as the first human ancestor.

A few years after the discovery of Lucy, British anthropologist Mary Leakey found a trail of footprint fossils in Tanzania in Africa. The fossil footprints seem to have been made by two hominids, walking side by side. Perhaps the larger hominid, the parent, was holding the hand of the smaller one, its offspring. Whatever else these fossil footprints show, they make one thing clear—whoever made them walked upright on two legs, as humans do. And, when the mud in which the footprints were embedded was analyzed, it was found to be about 4 million years old. This evidence showed that these hominids walked the Earth 4 million years ago!

Over the years, more hominid fossils have been discovered and placed in the genus *Australopithecus*. To date, there are two other species in addition to *A. africanus* and *A. afarensis*. They are *A. robustus* and *A. boisei*. Which species is actually the earliest ancestor of humans? Might an even younger fossil qualify instead, or perhaps an older fossil? Could the true human ancestor still be hidden somewhere in the Earth's soil? The debate and the search continue.

Fossil Evidence Versus Chemical Evidence

Until about 1970 evidence for human evolution had come primarily from fossils. Based on this evidence, most scientists estimated that apes and humans began to take separate evolutionary paths more than 14 million years ago.

In the 1970s, new laboratory evidence emerged to contradict this concept. A new method for measuring differences between the proteins of different species had been developed. Scientists had also developed a scale that could be used to estimate the rate of change in proteins over time. As you may recall from Chapter 2, this scale of protein change was referred to as a molecular clock.

In one case scientists compared the protein structures of hemoglobin in various modern primates, including humans. Hemoglobin is the red pigment in blood. The hemoglobin of humans and

Figure 3–10 *Based on the molecular clock, or scale of protein change, scientists determined that gorillas (right) took a separate evolutionary path before the paths of chimpanzees (left) and humans separated.*

chimpanzees had exactly the same sequence of 287 amino acids, which are the building blocks of proteins. The hemoglobin of humans and gorillas, however, differed in the position of 2 amino acids. This evidence led scientists to conclude that gorillas took a separate evolutionary path before the paths of chimpanzees and humans separated.

When did the gorilla path split off? According to the molecular clock, each change in the hemoglobin molecule would have taken 3 to 4 million years to occur. So gorillas would have taken a separate path 6 to 8 million years ago. Chimpanzees and humans would have taken separate paths more recently. This suggested split was much more recent than the 14-million-year date provided by fossil evidence. Today many scientists estimate that this split in evolutionary paths took place as recently as 2 million years ago.

Skillful Human: *Homo habilis*

The first species of hominid to actually be called human was also the maker of the first tools. *Homo habilis* (ha-BIH-lihs), which means skillful human, lived about 2 million years ago. The fossils of *Homo habilis* were first discovered in the 1960s in Olduvai Gorge in Kenya by the Leakey expedition. Olduvai Gorge is the oldest settlement of humans yet discovered.

In 1972, Kenyan anthropologist Louis Leakey (husband of Mary Leakey) reported the discovery of

Figure 3–11 *This skull of* Homo habilis, *which was found in Kenya, is about 1.8 million years old. The pebble tools, which are thought to be associated with* Homo habilis, *may have been used to prepare food.*

more fossils of *H. habilis.* These fossils included stone tools, such as the ones shown in Figure 3–11. These tools may have been used to prepare vegetables and to hunt smaller animals.

Upright Human: *Homo erectus*

The next humans known to scientists lived in caves, where they kept themselves safe from animals and from bad weather. These humans used fire to provide heat and light for their caves. Interestingly, however, these humans did not know how to build fires. So they waited until lightning set fire to a nearby bush, and then they carefully brought the fire back to their caves. Over the fire, they cooked the meat of animals and roasted nuts and seeds.

Along with fossils of these hominids, scientists have found carefully chipped hand axes. Painstaking examination of these tools has given scientists a good idea of how the tools were made. It may have happened something like this: Holding a small piece of sandstone in one hand, a hominid would strike the sandstone against a flat rock again and again, chipping off small pieces. These pieces were then gathered. If they happened to be the right size, they were rubbed into blades and points that were used to make weapons for hunting small animals.

This description is about all that is known of the life of the early human called *Homo erectus* (eh-REHK-tuhs). *H. erectus* lived from about 1.6 million to 500,000 years ago. *H. erectus* was the earliest human species to move out of Africa. Fossils of *H. erectus* have been found on the island of Java in Indonesia, near Heidelberg, Germany, and near Beijing, China. *H. erectus* had thicker bones than modern humans do, a sloping forehead, and a very large jaw. Such a large jaw would have been needed to chew some of the tough foods these humans ate. No one knows precisely what became of *H. erectus.*

Figure 3–12 Homo erectus *replaced* Homo habilis, *spreading throughout Europe, Africa, and Asia about 1 million years ago. Evidence strongly indicates that* Homo erectus *used and controlled fire.*

PROBLEM Solving ???

A Prehistoric Puzzle

Scientists have discovered fossils of *Homo erectus* in many places on Earth. In one site in Spain scientists were puzzled by a set of events. They found the remains of ancient brush fires on top of a cliff. At the base of the cliff they uncovered the bones of an entire herd of elephants. Scattered among the elephant bones were some stone tools.

Developing a Hypothesis

■ Suggest a hypothesis that would explain the events.

■ How can your hypothesis be used to explain the behavior of *Homo erectus*?

Wise Humans: *Homo sapiens*

About 500,000 years ago a new species of hominids appeared on Earth. Because the fossils of this new species had a body skeleton much like modern humans, as well as a brain of similar capacity, the species was called *Homo sapiens* (SAY-pee-ehnz), or wise human. There are three groups of *H. sapiens.* One group, which is called early *H. sapiens,* lived about 500,000 to 200,000 years ago. Unfortunately, because fossils of this group are scarce, scientists know very little about early *H. sapiens.* As you will soon learn, however, there is more fossil evidence concerning the remaining two groups of *H. sapiens.*

NEANDERTHALS The period from about 150,000 years ago to about 35,000 years ago produced an abundance of fossils of what are now called **Neanderthals.** Neanderthals, who lived in parts of Africa, Asia, and Europe, received their name from the Neander Valley in Germany, where their fossils were first discovered. They were given the genus and species *Homo neanderthalensis* (nee-AN-der-thawl-ehn-sihs). The species name *neanderthalensis* remained with these hominids for many years. The name was changed, however, when more complete fossil evidence came to light. This evidence indicated that although Neanderthals were more heavily built than modern humans are, they stood as erect as modern humans do and had a brain capacity as large as that of modern humans. Neanderthals fished and hunted birds and large animals. They also used handmade stone tools. As a result of all this evidence, Neanderthals were placed in the same species as

Figure 3–13 *This illustration shows two of the many theories about the trend of human evolution. What are the major differences between these two theories?*

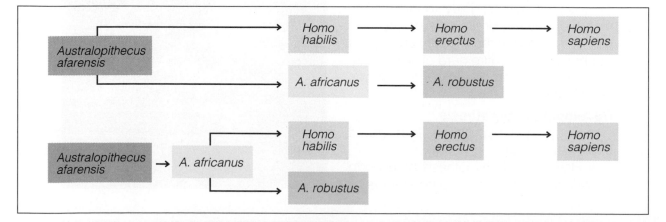

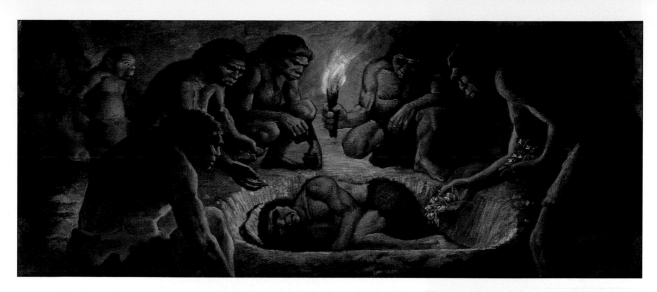

Figure 3–14 *Neanderthals are the oldest known hominids to have buried their dead with objects that include tools, animal bones, and even herbs.*

modern humans—*Homo sapiens*. But because Neanderthals were not truly identical to modern humans, the word *neanderthalensis* was added. So Neanderthals are now known as *Homo sapiens neanderthalensis*.

Although Neanderthals sometimes lived in caves, it is likely they moved from place to place in search of food. When Neanderthals camped out in the open, they probably built temporary huts by stretching animal skins over a framework of bones. The burnt wood found in Neanderthal camps suggests that they were experts at controlling fire. They may even have known how to start a fire with flint.

More impressive than the Neanderthals' ability to hunt, fish, cook, and make tools is the fact that they must have been the first hominids to act according to beliefs and feelings about the nature of the world. Like the ancient Egyptians, who lived many thousands of years later, Neanderthals buried their dead with the tools, herbs, or animal bones that had been important to the dead individuals in life. Sometimes the Neanderthals arranged animal bones around the graves in patterns that suggest religious rituals.

CRO-MAGNONS The first humans identical to modern humans began to appear on Earth about 40,000 years ago. These large-brained people were called **Cro-Magnons** (kroh-MAG-nuhnz), after the place in southwestern France where they were first discovered. However, similar fossils dating back 92,000 years ago have been found in Qafzeh, Israel.

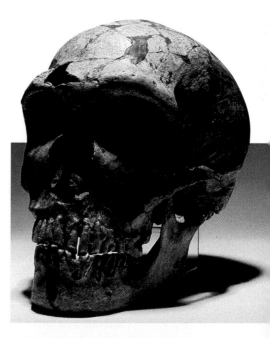

Figure 3–15 *This Neanderthal skull, which was found in France, is between 35,000 and 53,000 years old. The pattern of wear on the teeth indicates that the hominid probably used its teeth for more than eating—perhaps for softening hides.*

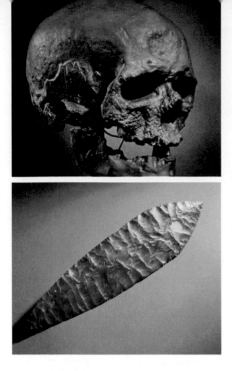

Figure 3–16 *Cro-Magnons, who were the first hominids truly identical to modern humans, appeared on Earth about 100,000 years ago. New and different tools, such as the laurel-leaf blade made from flint and used as the point of a spear, characterized their culture.*

Cro-Magnons were thinner than the Neanderthals were and had a more complex culture. Cro-Magnons also made more advanced tools, such as spears, fishing hooks, and needles. And, Cro-Magnons produced some of the most creative works of art in early human history. Cro-Magnons are now placed in the same group as modern humans are—*Homo sapiens sapiens*—meaning the wisest of the wise.

Scientists have carefully studied evidence that might provide additional clues to Cro-Magnon life. Such evidence indicates that Cro-Magnons worked together to make tools, build shelters, and hunt. To do so, they probably spoke to one another. Because they did not leave written records, no one has any idea what their language may have been like.

Whatever the language may have been, its importance for the future development of humans right up to today cannot be underestimated. Language is used to spread ideas. Although many animals communicate by sounds, only humans have developed a complicated communication system capable of transferring much of what goes on in one person's mind to that of another.

Language can be thought of as a final step in the evolution of the modern *H. sapiens sapiens*. Largely because of language, humans have developed a new characteristic: the ability to describe, or examine, one's own existence. As far as anyone knows, humans are the only animals capable of talking about themselves and of peering back down the long path of history to their own beginnings.

ACTIVITY

WRITING

The Iceman

Using reference materials in the library, find out about the 4000-year-old man discovered in September 1991 preserved in ice on the Similaun Glacier. This glacier is found in a pass between Austria and Italy. Describe the clothing that this prehistoric man wore and the significance of the bronze-headed ax he carried.

3–2 Section Review

1. What are some adaptations of human ancestors?
2. What evolutionary paths led to modern humans?
3. Which genus was the first hominid to walk upright?

Critical Thinking—*Relating Facts*

4. Suppose you were able to meet a group that consisted of the following: *Homo erectus, Homo sapiens sapiens, Homo sapiens neanderthalensis*, Lucy, and *Australopithecus africanus*. How would you distinguish one from the other?

Dating a Neanderthal

In early 1991, at an archaeological site near the village of St.-Césaire, north of Bordeaux, France, scientists discovered a Neanderthal skeleton. The fossil provided evidence that Neanderthals lived in Western Europe as recently as 36,000 years ago. This date is several thousand years after the first modern humans were believed to have appeared there.

How were the scientists able to determine the age of the fossil? Because the usual technique of radiocarbon dating is not effective with objects so old, scientists had to use another method of dating. The technique the scientists employed is called *thermoluminescence* (ther-moh-loo-muh-NEHS-ehns), and it was used on the flint tools found with the skeleton. Thermoluminescence involves the study of the *light energy* released when flint is heated to a temperature of about 450°C. By heating the flint to this temperature, the electrons (negatively charged particles) in the atoms of the flint are rearranged. Their changes in position release energy. The amount of energy released is analyzed to determine how much time has passed since the flint was last heated.

In this case, thermoluminescence showed that the age of the flint tools was about 36,300 years, give or take 2700 years. From this evidence, the scientists concluded that the bones of the Neanderthal skeleton were the same age as the flint tools. A fossil skeleton of the most recent Neanderthal yet known had been identified using energy in the forms of heat and light.

Laboratory Investigation

Comparing Primates—From Gorillas to Humans

Problem

What changes occurred as humans evolved from earlier primates?

Materials *(per student)*

scissors	metric ruler
clean paper	protractor

Procedure

1. Insert a 6 cm X 9 cm strip of paper lengthwise into your mouth. Place the paper over your tongue so that it covers all your teeth, including your back molars. Bite down hard enough to make an impression of your teeth on the paper. Remove the paper from your mouth.

2. Draw a line on the paper from the center of the impression of the left back molar to the center of the impression of the right back molar. Mark the midpoint of this line. Use the protractor to draw a perpendicular line from the midpoint of the line connecting the back molars to the front teeth.

3. Measure the width of the jaw by measuring the length of the line between the back molars. Measure the length of the jaw by measuring the line from the back of the mouth to the front teeth. Record your measurements in a data table.

4. Calculate the jaw index by multiplying the jaw width by 100 and then dividing by the length of the jaw. Record the jaw index.

5. Repeat steps 3 and 4 using the drawings of gorilla and *Australopithecus* jaws.

6. Find the indentation at the bottom of your palm near the ball of your thumb. Measure the length of your thumb from the indentation to its tip. Measure the length of

your index finger from the indentation to its tip. Record these measurements.

7. Calculate the thumb index by multiplying the thumb length by 100. Divide by the index-finger length. Record the thumb index.

8. Repeat steps 6 and 7 using the drawings of the thumb and index finger of both the gorilla and *Australopithecus*.

Observations

What trend did you observe regarding the relative length of the jaw? The relative length of the thumb and index finger?

Analysis and Conclusions

1. Was *Australopithecus* a mammal with characteristics somewhere in between those of gorillas and humans? Give evidence to support your answer.

2. Based on the thumb index, what adaptive change occurred in human evolution? What was the advantage of this change?

3. Based on your observations, what other change occurred as humans evolved?

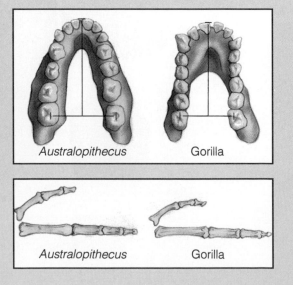

Australopithecus   Gorilla

Australopithecus   Gorilla

Summarizing Key Concepts

3–1 The Search for Human Ancestors

▲ Primates are members of a group of mammals that includes humans, monkeys, and about 200 other species of living things.

▲ Primates share several important characteristics: They have flexible hands with opposable thumbs; they can see in three dimensions; and they have large, complex cerebrums.

▲ Some 50 million years ago, early primates split into two main evolutionary groups: prosimians and anthropoids.

▲ The anthropoids then split into two branches. One branch evolved into New World monkeys. The other branch evolved into Old World monkeys and hominoids; hominoids include gorillas, gibbons, orangutans, chimpanzees, and humans.

3–2 Human Ancestors and Relatives

▲ About 6 million years ago, hominoids gave rise to a small group of species called hominids, which include humans and closely related primates.

▲ Early hominids experienced changes in the shapes of their spinal column and their hip and leg bones. These changes enabled them to walk upright and thus freed their hands to use tools. At the same time the opposable thumb evolved.

▲ The first recognized hominids were called *Australopithecus.*

▲ Chemical and fossil evidence indicates that the split between apes and humans may have occurred 2 million years ago.

▲ The first species to be placed in the genus *Homo* was skillful human, or *Homo habilis.*

▲ *Homo habilis* was followed by *Homo erectus.*

▲ The first species to resemble modern humans seems to have evolved 150,000 years ago and is called *Homo sapiens neanderthalensis.*

▲ The first fossils of modern humans date to about 100,000 years ago. These humans, called Cro-Magnons, are in the genus *Homo sapiens sapiens,* as are modern humans.

Reviewing Key Terms

Define each term in a complete sentence.

3–1 The Search for Human Ancestors
primate

3–2 Human Ancestors and Relatives
Neanderthal
Cro-Magnon

Chapter Review

Content Review

Multiple Choice

Choose the letter of the answer that best completes each statement.

1. Which does not include humans, apes, and monkeys?
   a. mammals   c. primates
   b. vertebrates   d. *Homo sapiens*

2. Which is not a characteristic of all primates?
   a. three-dimensional vision
   b. flexible hands
   c. two-legged walking
   d. larger cerebrum

3. What characteristic do humans have that other primates do not?
   a. sharp vision
   b. three-dimensional vision
   c. two-legged walking
   d. opposable thumbs

4. The molecular clock is used to study changes in
   a. proteins.   c. muscle tissue.
   b. bones.   d. brain size.

5. The humans who first skillfully made tools were
   a. *Australopithecus africanus.*
   b. *Homo sapiens.*
   c. *Homo habilis.*
   d. *Homo erectus.*

6. The first humans known to bury their dead were
   a. *Homo habilis.*   c. Neanderthals.
   b. *Homo erectus.*   d. Cro-Magnons.

7. Humans that could control fire were
   a. Neanderthals.
   b. *Homo habilis.*
   c. *Homo erectus.*
   d. *Australopithecus africanus.*

8. The first humans believed to have used language were
   a. *Homo habilis.*   c. *Homo erectus.*
   b. *A. africanus.*   d. Cro-Magnons.

True or False

If the statement is true, write "true." If it is false, change the underlined word or words to make the statement true.

1. <u>Hominids</u> are a group of mammals that includes humans, apes, and monkeys.
2. Gibbons and chimpanzees are examples of <u>New World</u> monkeys.
3. <u>Louis Leakey</u> discovered the first fossil of a hominid and named it *Australopithecus*.
4. The humanlike fossil nicknamed Lucy is about <u>14</u> million years old.
5. *Homo habilis* means <u>upright</u> human.
6. Primitive huts have been found in <u>Neanderthal</u> campsites.
7. <u>Cro-Magnon</u> is included in the species *Homo sapiens sapiens*.

Concept Mapping

Complete the following concept map for Section 3–1. Refer to pages F6–F7 to construct a concept map for the entire chapter.

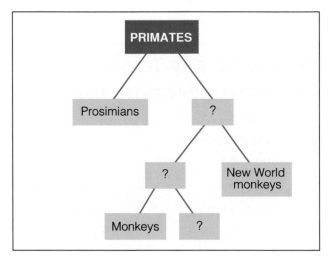

Concept Mastery

Discuss each of the following in a brief paragraph.

1. Describe the characteristics of primates. Explain how humans are different from other primates.
2. Explain how a blending of Neanderthals and Cro-Magnons could have led to modern humans.
3. Explain how protein structures are used to measure differences between species. Include a definition of molecular clock in your explanation.
4. Compare *H. habilis* and *H. erectus.*

5. Compare *Australopithecus afarensis* with *Australopithecus africanus.*
6. Explain how Neanderthals and Cro-Magnons differ.
7. Discuss the benefits that result from the ability to use language.
8. Compare anthropoids, hominoids, and hominids.
9. Discuss possible reasons for the disappearance of the Neanderthals.

Critical Thinking and Problem Solving

Use the skills you have developed in this chapter to complete each of the following.

1. **Interpreting graphs** Another characteristic that distinguishes humans from other primates is the length of time parents care for their young. The graph illustrates the length of time needed for three different species of primates to reach adulthood. Use the graph to answer the following questions.
   a. Which organism has the shortest preadult stage? The longest?
   b. How is the length of the preadult stage related to the intelligence of each primate species?

2. **Relating concepts** People often say that evolution means that humans evolved from monkeys and apes. Explain why such a statement is not an accurate representation of human evolution.
3. **Relating facts** Explain how the characteristics of primates made them successful at living in trees.
4. **Making comparisons** What advantages does a primate with the ability to walk on two legs have over a primate that walks on four legs?
5. **Relating concepts** How is the ability to learn language related to the development of human civilizations?
6. **Applying concepts** Do you think evolution on Earth has stopped? If not, do you think evolution will ever stop? Explain your answers.
7. **Using the writing process** With the exception of modern humans after the time of Cro-Magnon, choose a hominid and write a short story entitled "A Day in the Life of a Hominid."

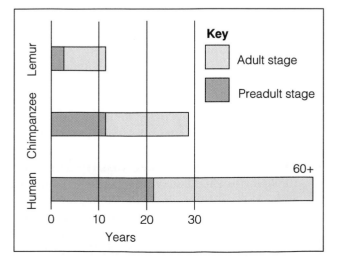

Jack Horner Warms Up To Dinosaurs

Paleontologist Jack Horner is not interested in how dinosaurs died. Rather, he is interested in how they lived.

Horner, who teaches at Montana State University and is also curator of paleontology at the Museum of the Rockies in Bozeman, Montana, heads the largest dinosaur research team in the United States. His work focuses on the behavior of dinosaurs, and his research findings are considered quite revolutionary. You see, Horner has discovered that these extinct creatures were not always the enormous, bloodthirsty monsters portrayed in horror movies and popular cartoons. More likely, Horner says, many dinosaurs were social plant-eaters and nurturing parents.

Horner's conclusions are based largely on research he has done in an area called the Willow Creek Anticline in his home state of Montana. He worked there for many years, uncovering fossils that date back to the Cretaceous Period, some 65 to 135 million years ago.

In studying the dinosaurs, Horner is ful-

filling a goal he has had since he discovered his first fossil at age eight. Throughout high school, he knew he wanted to be a paleontologist. But his schoolwork was rather poor and remained so throughout his college experience. (He flunked out of college seven times.) However, he continued taking and excelling in courses in paleontology, eventually earning an assistantship in paleontology at Princeton University. At age 31, while at Princeton, Horner discovered his academic problems were the result of dyslexia. Dyslexia is a condition in which the ability to read is impaired.

While still at Princeton, Horner became particularly fascinated with the study of juvenile dinosaurs—an area of paleontology that had received little or no attention. His fascination took him back to Montana where, quite by accident, he stumbled upon a collection of dinosaur egg fossils. The events leading to this discovery occurred something like this: While traveling through his native state in the late 1970s, Horner and a friend decided to stop for a brief rest at a small shop where rocks were sold. The owner, an amateur fossil collector, asked Horner to identify some bones she had found. Upon close examination, Horner was amazed to see that the collection included some bone fragments from baby hadrosaurs, or duck-bill dinosaurs. No sooner had the shopowner showed Horner where she had found the fossils, than he began to dig.

Working at the Willow Creek Anticline through the 1980s, Horner and his team unearthed many dinosaur eggs and skeletons of young dinosaurs, particularly those of hadrosaurs. The shape and texture of the egg shells, as well as the structure of the baby dinosaur skulls, led Horner to some new and exciting conclusions about the behavior of hadrosaurs. Baby hadrosaurs, Horner says, kept their babylike features—large heads with big eyes and shortened snouts—throughout their lives. These features encouraged adult dinosaurs to nurture them. Adult hadrosaurs, Horner believes, guarded their eggs before they hatched and then fed and protected their young after they were born. He has even given a name to the genus of dinosaur he discovered with these nurturing traits. He calls the genus *Maiasaura*, meaning good mother dinosaur.

Horner brings the past into view of the present and uses the latest techniques of the present to study the past. As curator of paleontology at the Museum of the Rockies, Horner wants his visitors to see how he believes dinosaurs lived during their 140-million-year reign on Earth. For example, he designs his displays to show dinosaurs doing such ordinary actions as scratching their jaws and sitting calmly on the ground. Horner has also coauthored a book on—what else?—dinosaurs. In addition, he is a consultant for a Japanese amusement park that

▲ **A duckbilled adult oversees a nest of newly hatched maiasaurs. The hatchlings are tended to for months by adults.**

has a huge display—complete with robot models—of the history of Earth.

Horner, the former college dropout, is now well into his forties. The years of struggling with dyslexia have not prevented him from earning the respect of fellow scientists, as well as the prestigious MacArthur Foundation fellowship. Interestingly, this award is also known as the "genius award."

FROM RULERS TO RUINS:
The Death of the Dinosaurs

They were lords of the Earth for over 135 million years— giant reptiles that thrived in the mild climate of prehistoric Earth, with its warm waters and lush foliage. Then suddenly, 65 million years ago, these unchallenged rulers of the planet disappeared completely. The great dinosaurs became extinct!

Imagine what the last days of the dinosaurs might have been like. . . . A *Triceratops* munches peacefully on a clump of green bushes. Nearby a baby *Stegosaurus* runs frantically from the deadly jaws of the *Tyrannosaurus*, king of the flesh-eating dinosaurs. A long-necked *Brontosaurus* wades into a pond as a *Pterodactyl* flies overhead. None of these animals notices the dark shadow that begins to move across the land. The shadow grows larger as a huge rock, the size of a mountain, blocks the sun.

The rock is hurtling toward Earth. When it strikes, a deafening boom and tremendous earthquakes shake the land. The heat generated by the collision starts fires that rage through the tropical forests. At the same time, the violent impact sends a mushroom-shaped cloud of dust into the atmosphere. The dust combines with the smoke and ash from the forest fires to form a thick blanket that spreads across the globe and blots out the sun.

For several months or longer, the huge dust cloud hovers in the atmosphere, preventing sunlight from reaching Earth. The Earth becomes a dark, cold planet. Plants, which rely on sunlight to make their food, begin to die off. Plant-eating dinosaurs now have nothing to eat, and they too begin to die. And flesh-eating dinosaurs can no longer find nourishment. In all, almost 96 percent of all plant and animal species are killed during this time period!

This theory to explain the extinction of the dinosaurs is known as the asteroid-impact theory. Luis and Walter Alvarez, the father-and-son team from California responsible for the theory, have suggested that a large asteroid, perhaps 10 kilometers in diameter, struck Earth about 65 million years ago and began the chain of events you have just read.

The Alvarezes have evidence to support their theory. They have studied the layers of clay formed during the time of the dinosaur extinction. In the clay, they have found high levels of iridium, an element that is extremely rare on Earth. Their readings show levels of iridium 160 times greater than normal. Where could the iridium have come from?

The Alvarezes believe asteroids from outer space are the source. Asteroids are known to contain high levels of iridium. According to the asteroid-impact theory, iridium was deposited in the clay when the asteroid struck Earth and set off the series of events that killed the dinosaurs.

Although the evidence of iridium in the clay seems convincing, not all scientists agree with the theory. Critics say that the high levels of iridium can be traced to volcanic

eruptions, which bring iridium buried deep within the Earth to the surface and release it into the atmosphere.

But further study of the clay and sediment layers from the time of the dinosaur extinction continues to yield evidence supporting the asteroid-impact theory. Geologists have found quartz from the ancient sediment that contains cracks that could be the result of a single huge impact—such as the impact of an asteroid. Also, chemists have discovered in the clay a form of an amino acid that is almost nonexistent on Earth. It is, however, common in meteors.

Still, the debate continues. Some scientists protest that the extinction of the dinosaurs did not happen all of a sudden. They believe that the dinosaurs died out gradually due to changes in climate and sea level. The scientists support their claims with fossil evidence. Paleontologists have found dinosaur bones and eggs in sediment and clay layers formed nearly 64 million years ago. This is one million years after the asteroid-impact theory claims all the dinosaurs should have become extinct.

Gradual extinction of the dinosaurs could have been the result of major climate changes on the Earth over several million years. Many scientists think the Earth's temperature cooled dramatically around the time of dinosaur extinction. The resulting death of

plant life in turn led to the gradual downfall of the dinosaurs.

Still other scientists believe that the development of small furry mammals might have contributed to the dinosaurs' end. Tiny clever rodents that were able to outrun and outsmart the huge dinosaurs could have eaten the dinosaurs' eggs. As time passed, older dinosaurs would die and fewer young dinosaurs would be born, leading to the dinosaurs' extinction.

Recent findings have shown that the level of oxygen in the Earth's atmosphere during the time of the dinosaurs was much higher than it was in the periods following their extinction. Although this clue must still be studied in more depth before any conclusions are drawn, scientists are hopeful that this discovery will shed new light on the question of dinosaur extinction.

The factors that caused the downfall of the great dinosaurs are quite complex. Did an asteroid falling from space kill off the giant reptiles? Was it a change in climate or perhaps even a worldwide disease that destroyed the largest land creatures ever to walk the Earth? Could it have been tiny furry mammals that spelled doom for the dinosaurs? Perhaps a combination of all these factors brought about dinosaur extinction. What do you think?

SCIENCE GAZETTE:

EVOLUTION
ON VIVARIUM

The rules of evolution, if followed elsewhere in space, may have produced living things undreamed of on Earth.

FROM: *Dr. Toshi Kanamoto, Bio-Ship 80*
TO: *Dr. Peter Harrington, Command Station 40, Earth*
RE: *Life on Planet Vivarium*

Greetings Pete:
　　We are now orbiting the planet Vivarium and are T minus 3 hours 20 minutes to landing. In just 3 more hours, if all goes well, we should be the first Earthlings to touch down on Vivarium.

You can imagine the excitement I feel. According to the data we received from the last exploratory satellite, the atmosphere of Vivarium is rich in oxygen. In fact, there is more than enough oxygen to sustain life as we know it on Earth.

Dr. Susan Haley, our ship's anthropologist, and Captain Jasper Fernandez, our commander, are angry with me. I just showed them the photograph I had been holding of the ET, or extraterrestrial life form. The photograph was taken on Vivarium by the satellite we sent out six months ago. Both

of Vivarium's atmosphere. Haley argued that the slits were sense organs, probably eyes. She contended that eyes would be an important adaptation to the rocky, lake-filled terrain of Vivarium.

I suggested that we consider some other senses that might be adaptations on Vivarium. Haley and Fernandez looked at me curiously. Finally Fernandez said, "Go on."

"Well, we know that each hemisphere of Vivarium is in semidarkness part of each year," I reasoned. "Could the creature have evolved a way of seeing by means of heat waves, rather than light waves, to help it live in the dark?"

feel it was wrong of me to keep the photograph a secret until now. But I knew the photograph would create a storm of controversy among the three of us. I just wanted to avoid spending ten days in space arguing over what the photograph tells us. But I'm afraid Haley and Fernandez disagree with my reasoning.

The photograph of the ET shows what looks like the head of a land creature, at the edge of a lake. The head is shaped something like that of an ant. Fernandez, Haley, and I immediately agreed that its black, smooth "skin" is probably an exoskeleton, or outer skeleton. This would be similar to the exoskeletons of some of Earth's insects.

Haley and Fernandez next began to discuss the three slits on the surface of the creature's head, above the mouth. Fernandez insisted that all three openings were breathing holes. They would allow the creature to take advantage of the rich oxygen content

Haley and Fernandez were impressed with my hypothesis and urged me to continue.

"Let's not forget about the radioactive ores our satellite discovered on Vivarium. Maybe the creature has evolved a sense that is like a biological Geiger counter. This sense would warn the creature whenever it came near dangerous concentrations of radioactivity."

"Those are two strong possibilities," said Haley. She began scanning the photograph closely. "I wonder how big the ET is. If this is only the head, the entire creature may be three times this size."

Fernandez and I tripled the head proportions, took the scale of the photograph into account, and figured that the creature was more than 200 times larger than any insect on Earth. But Haley insisted that our calculations had to be wrong. She wanted to know how such a gigantic creature could possibly support its own mass. It would be impossible for an exoskeleton to withstand so much stress."

"At any rate," she said, "the creature would need elephant-sized, rather than insect-sized, legs to support such a mass."

Before Haley could continue, Fernandez reminded her of an important difference between Vivarium and Earth. The surface gravity of Vivarium is only one quarter that of Earth. This would allow for the evolution of a creature with a more massive body and thinner legs.

"All right," said Haley, "but you've got to admit, such a bulky creature would need at least six legs for balance. We have to picture it making its way over the rocky, uneven terrain of Vivarium in near darkness."

"Why stop at six legs?" I said. "And why consider only legs?" Again the two looked at me expectantly.

"According to the data brought back by our satellite," I went on, "the craters and canyons of Vivarium are covered with a thin film of water at least part of the year. Perhaps the wet, slippery rocks of this planet require the creature to have suction cups instead of legs and feet. Perhaps the crea-

ture's body is covered with suction cups so it could move even if it rolled over."

By the time our discussion drew to a close, it was clear to me that we can only make educated guesses about evolution on other planets. The guesses, of course, would be based on our knowledge of the environment of the planet. We had turned the ET into a creature that was the size of an elephant and had a head and outer skeleton that were similar to those of an ant. It had suction cups covering its body, and the ability to sense changes in heat and radiation levels.

I left Haley and Fernandez arguing about the creature's probable lung capacity. I was glad that I had decided to delay the battle over the ET. As it was, our discussion had taken up the last 3 hours of the voyage.

Well, Pete, I'm afraid I must sign off now. I can hear the first landing rockets firing. I wanted to get all of our ET discussion recorded before touchdown. Vivarium may very well prove to be the testing ground for a great many of our hypotheses about evolution on other planets. If everything goes as I expect it will, my next letter should make for some very exciting reading.

For Further Reading

If you have been intrigued by the concepts examined in this textbook, you may also be interested in the ways fellow thinkers—novelists, poets, essayists, as well as scientists—have imaginatively explored the same ideas.

Chapter 1: Earth's History in Fossils

Anker, Charlotte. *Last Night I Saw Andromeda.* New York: Henry Z. Walck, Inc.

Conrad, Pam. *My Daniel.* New York: Harper & Row.

Katz, Welwyn Wilton. *False Face.* New York: Margaret K. McElderry Books.

Kelleher, Victor. *Baily's Bones.* New York: Dial Press.

Chapter 2: Changes in Living Things Over Time

Boulle, Pierre. *Planet of the Apes.* New York: Vanguard.

Dickinson, Peter. *Box of Nothing.* New York: Delacorte Press.

Lord, Bette Bao. *In the Year of the Boar and Jackie Robinson.* New York: Harper & Row.

Niven, Larry and Jerry Pournelle. *The Mote in God's Eye.* New York: Pocket Books.

Chapter 3: The Path to Modern Humans

Denzel, Justin. *Boy of the Painted Cave.* New York: Philomel Books.

Dyer, T. A. *A Way of His Own.* Boston, MA: Houghton Mifflin Co.

L'Engle, Madeleine. *Many Waters.* New York: Farrar, Straus, Giroux.

Millstead, Thomas. *Cave of the Moving Shadows.* New York: Dial Press.

Activity Bank

Welcome to the Activity Bank! This is an exciting and enjoyable part of your science textbook. By using the Activity Bank you will have the chance to make a variety of interesting and different observations about science. The best thing about the Activity Bank is that you and your classmates will become the detectives, and as with any investigation you will have to sort through information to find the truth. There will be many twists and turns along the way, some surprises and disappointments too. So always remember to keep an open mind, ask lots of questions, and have fun learning about science.

WHERE ARE THEY?

Natural selection is the survival and reproduction of those living things best adapted to their surroundings. To better understand how natural selection works, why not try this activity on camouflage, or the ability of living things to blend in with their background.

What Will You Need?

hole punch

colored construction paper (1 sheet of each of the following colors: black, blue, brown, green, orange, purple, red, white, yellow)

9 sealable plastic bags

80 cm × 80 cm piece of floral paper or cloth

transparent tape

What Will You Do?

1. Punch 10 dots of each color from the sheets of colored construction paper. Put the dots for each color in a different plastic bag.

2. Spread a piece of floral paper or cloth on a flat surface. Use transparent tape to attach each corner of the paper or cloth to the flat surface.

3. Choose one member of your group to be the recorder and another to be the predator. The other members of the group will be the prey.

4. Have the predator look away while the prey randomly spread the dots of each color over the paper.

Hole punch

Sealable plastic bags

Construction paper

Piece of floral paper

Transparent tape

5. Have the predator turn back to the paper and immediately pick up the first dot he or she sees.

Spreading the Dots

Picking up the Dots

6. Repeat steps 4 and 5 until a total of 10 dots have been picked up. Make sure that the predator looks away before a selection is made each time.

7. In a data table similar to the one shown, have the recorder write the total number of dots selected by the predator next to the appropriate color.

8. Have the recorder and the predator reverse roles. Repeat steps 4 through 7.

9. On posterboard, construct a data table similar to yours. Have your classmates record their results in this data table.

What Will You See?

DATA TABLE

Color of Dots	Number of Dots Selected
Black	
Blue	
Brown	
Green	
Orange	
Purple	
Red	
White	
Yellow	

What Will You Discover?

1. Which colored dots were picked up from the floral background?

2. Which colored dots, if any, were not picked up? Explain.

3. How did your results compare with your classmates' results?

4. If the colored dots represent food to a predator, what is the advantage of camouflage?

5. If the colored dots (prey) were to pass through several generations, what trends in survival of prey would you observe?

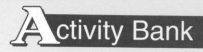
VARIETY IS THE SPICE OF LIFE

The fossil record shows that living things have evolved, or changed over time. How do these changes produce complex living things from simple ones? How can one group of living things evolve into many different groups? How can you show these changes in the form of an evolutionary tree (diagram that shows the evolutionary relationships among different groups of living things)? To find out the answers to these questions, try this activity. You will need the following materials: sheets of construction paper (red, blue, green, and black), metric ruler, scissors, posterboard, glue, pencil, compass.

What You Will Do

1. With the scissors, cut out 12 4-cm squares from a sheet of green construction paper.

2. Cut out one 4-cm square from a sheet of black construction paper. Then cut the square in half diagonally so that you have two black triangles. Put one triangle aside for now and discard the other.

3. Repeat step 2 using a sheet of red construction paper.

4. With a compass, draw a circle that has a diameter of 4 cm on a sheet of blue construction paper. Put the blue circle aside for now.

5. Place the posterboard vertically on a flat surface. Draw a very faint line down the center of the posterboard.

6. Place one green square in the middle of the left side of the posterboard, about 5 cm from the bottom. Glue the green square in place.

7. Arrange 10 of the remaining green squares on the posterboard exactly as shown in the diagram on the left on page F109. You should have five rows of green squares: 1 square in the first row, 2 squares in the second and third rows, 3 squares in the fourth and fifth rows. Glue the squares in place.

8. Draw the arrows in as shown.

9. Go to the fifth row of green squares. Place the blue circle on top of the first green square so that it covers the square. Glue the blue circle in place.

10. On top of the middle green square in the fifth row, place the red triangle as shown in the diagram on the right on page F109. Glue the red triangle in place.

11. Above the third green square in the fifth row, place the last remaining green square so that you form a rectangle 8 cm × 4 cm. Then place the black triangle on top of the newly added fourth square. Glue the black triangle in place.

Construction paper

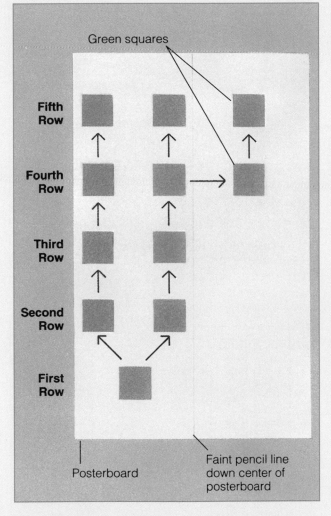

Green squares

Fifth Row

Fourth Row

Third Row

Second Row

First Row

Posterboard

Faint pencil line down center of posterboard

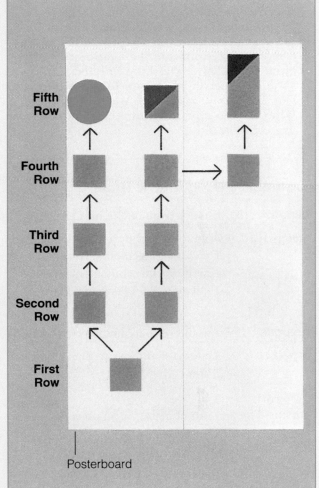

Fifth Row

Fourth Row

Third Row

Second Row

First Row

Posterboard

12. Observe the first row and the last row. Using the remaining sheets of colored construction paper, cut out the shapes that you think are needed to show the gradual change in shapes between the first row and the last row.

What You Will Discover

1. How does each row in your evolutionary tree compare with the row below it? With the row above it?

2. What relationship does this activity have with evolution?

3. Compare your evolutionary tree with those of your classmates. Are they the same? Are they different? Explain your answer.

Going Further

Replace the shapes in this activity with drawings of living things.

$\mathbb{A}$ppendix A

The metric system of measurement is used by scientists throughout the world. It is based on units of ten. Each unit is ten times larger or ten times smaller than the next unit. The most commonly used units of the metric system are given below. After you have finished reading about the metric system, try to put it to use. How tall are you in metrics? What is your mass? What is your normal body temperature in degrees Celsius?

Commonly Used Metric Units

Length   The distance from one point to another

meter (m)   A meter is slightly longer than a yard.
                1 meter = 1000 millimeters (mm)
                1 meter = 100 centimeters (cm)
                1000 meters = 1 kilometer (km)

Volume   The amount of space an object takes up

liter (L)   A liter is slightly more than a quart.
                1 liter = 1000 milliliters (mL)

Mass   The amount of matter in an object

gram (g)   A gram has a mass equal to about one paper clip.

                1000 grams = 1 kilogram (kg)

Temperature   The measure of hotness or coldness

degrees   0°C = freezing point of water
Celsius (°C)   100°C = boiling point of water

Metric–English Equivalents

2.54 centimeters (cm) = 1 inch (in.)
1 meter (m) = 39.37 inches (in.)
1 kilometer (km) = 0.62 miles (mi)
1 liter (L) = 1.06 quarts (qt)
250 milliliters (mL) = 1 cup (c)
1 kilogram (kg) = 2.2 pounds (lb)
28.3 grams (g) = 1 ounce (oz)
°C = 5/9 × (°F − 32)

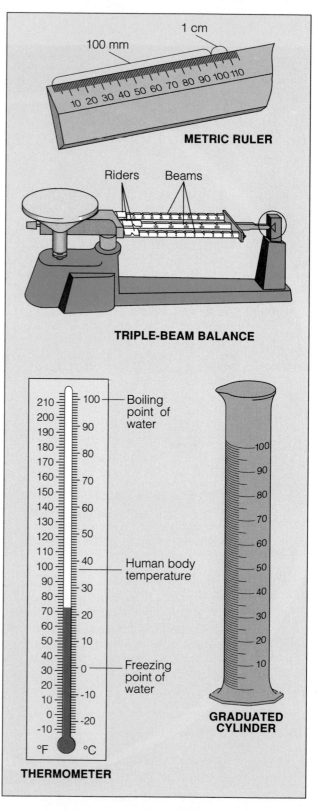

METRIC RULER

TRIPLE-BEAM BALANCE

THERMOMETER

GRADUATED CYLINDER

Glassware Safety

1. Whenever you see this symbol, you will know that you are working with glassware that can easily be broken. Take particular care to handle such glassware safely. And never use broken or chipped glassware.
2. Never heat glassware that is not thoroughly dry. Never pick up any glassware unless you are sure it is not hot. If it is hot, use heat-resistant gloves.
3. Always clean glassware thoroughly before putting it away.

Fire Safety

1. Whenever you see this symbol, you will know that you are working with fire. Never use any source of fire without wearing safety goggles.
2. Never heat anything—particularly chemicals—unless instructed to do so.
3. Never heat anything in a closed container.
4. Never reach across a flame.
5. Always use a clamp, tongs, or heat-resistant gloves to handle hot objects.
6. Always maintain a clean work area, particularly when using a flame.

Heat Safety

Whenever you see this symbol, you will know that you should put on heat-resistant gloves to avoid burning your hands.

Chemical Safety

1. Whenever you see this symbol, you will know that you are working with chemicals that could be hazardous.
2. Never smell any chemical directly from its container. Always use your hand to waft some of the odors from the top of the container toward your nose—and only when instructed to do so.
3. Never mix chemicals unless instructed to do so.
4. Never touch or taste any chemical unless instructed to do so.
5. Keep all lids closed when chemicals are not in use. Dispose of all chemicals as instructed by your teacher.

6. Immediately rinse with water any chemicals, particularly acids, that get on your skin and clothes. Then notify your teacher.

Eye and Face Safety

1. Whenever you see this symbol, you will know that you are performing an experiment in which you must take precautions to protect your eyes and face by wearing safety goggles.
2. When you are heating a test tube or bottle, always point it away from you and others. Chemicals can splash or boil out of a heated test tube.

Sharp Instrument Safety

1. Whenever you see this symbol, you will know that you are working with a sharp instrument.
2. Always use single-edged razors; double-edged razors are too dangerous.
3. Handle any sharp instrument with extreme care. Never cut any material toward you; always cut away from you.
4. Immediately notify your teacher if your skin is cut.

Electrical Safety

1. Whenever you see this symbol, you will know that you are using electricity in the laboratory.
2. Never use long extension cords to plug in any electrical device. Do not plug too many appliances into one socket or you may overload the socket and cause a fire.
3. Never touch an electrical appliance or outlet with wet hands.

Animal Safety

1. Whenever you see this symbol, you will know that you are working with live animals.
2. Do not cause pain, discomfort, or injury to an animal.
3. Follow your teacher's directions when handling animals. Wash your hands thoroughly after handling animals or their cages.

One of the first things a scientist learns is that working in the laboratory can be an exciting experience. But the laboratory can also be quite dangerous if proper safety rules are not followed at all times. To prepare yourself for a safe year in the laboratory, read over the following safety rules. Then read them a second time. Make sure you understand each rule. If you do not, ask your teacher to explain any rules you are unsure of.

Dress Code

1. Many materials in the laboratory can cause eye injury. To protect yourself from possible injury, wear safety goggles whenever you are working with chemicals, burners, or any substance that might get into your eyes. Never wear contact lenses in the laboratory.

2. Wear a laboratory apron or coat whenever you are working with chemicals or heated substances.

3. Tie back long hair to keep it away from any chemicals, burners and candles, or other laboratory equipment.

4. Remove or tie back any article of clothing or jewelry that can hang down and touch chemicals and flames.

General Safety Rules

5. Read all directions for an experiment several times. Follow the directions exactly as they are written. If you are in doubt about any part of the experiment, ask your teacher for assistance.

6. Never perform activities that are not authorized by your teacher. Obtain permission before "experimenting" on your own.

7. Never handle any equipment unless you have specific permission.

8. Take extreme care not to spill any material in the laboratory. If a spill occurs, immediately ask your teacher about the proper cleanup procedure. Never simply pour chemicals or other substances into the sink or trash container.

9. Never eat in the laboratory.

10. Wash your hands before and after each experiment.

First Aid

11. Immediately report all accidents, no matter how minor, to your teacher.

12. Learn what to do in case of specific accidents, such as getting acid in your eyes or on your skin. (Rinse acids from your body with lots of water.)

13. Become aware of the location of the first-aid kit. But your teacher should administer any required first aid due to injury. Or your teacher may send you to the school nurse or call a physician.

14. Know where and how to report an accident or fire. Find out the location of the fire extinguisher, phone, and fire alarm. Keep a list of important phone numbers—such as the fire department and the school nurse—near the phone. Immediately report any fires to your teacher.

Heating and Fire Safety

15. Again, never use a heat source, such as a candle or burner, without wearing safety goggles.

16. Never heat a chemical you are not instructed to heat. A chemical that is harmless when cool may be dangerous when heated.

17. Maintain a clean work area and keep all materials away from flames.

18. Never reach across a flame.

19. Make sure you know how to light a Bunsen burner. (Your teacher will demonstrate the proper procedure for lighting a burner.) If the flame leaps out of a burner toward you, immediately turn off the gas. Do not touch the burner. It may be hot. And never leave a lighted burner unattended!

20. When heating a test tube or bottle, always point it away from you and others. Chemicals can splash or boil out of a heated test tube.

21. Never heat a liquid in a closed container. The expanding gases produced may blow the container apart, injuring you or others.

22. Before picking up a container that has been heated, first hold the back of your hand near it. If you can feel the heat on the back of your hand, the container may be too hot to handle. Use a clamp or tongs when handling hot containers.

Using Chemicals Safely

23. Never mix chemicals for the "fun of it." You might produce a dangerous, possibly explosive substance.

24. Never touch, taste, or smell a chemical unless you are instructed by your teacher to do so. Many chemicals are poisonous. If you are instructed to note the fumes in an experiment, gently wave your hand over the opening of a container and direct the fumes toward your nose. Do not inhale the fumes directly from the container.

25. Use only those chemicals needed in the activity. Keep all lids closed when a chemical is not being used. Notify your teacher whenever chemicals are spilled.

26. Dispose of all chemicals as instructed by your teacher. To avoid contamination, never return chemicals to their original containers.

27. Be extra careful when working with acids or bases. Pour such chemicals over the sink, not over your workbench.

28. When diluting an acid, pour the acid into water. Never pour water into an acid.

29. Immediately rinse with water any acids that get on your skin or clothing. Then notify your teacher of any acid spill.

Using Glassware Safely

30. Never force glass tubing into a rubber stopper. A turning motion and lubricant will be helpful when inserting glass tubing into rubber stoppers or rubber tubing. Your teacher will demonstrate the proper way to insert glass tubing.

31. Never heat glassware that is not thoroughly dry. Use a wire screen to protect glassware from any flame.

32. Keep in mind that hot glassware will not appear hot. Never pick up glassware without first checking to see if it is hot. See #22.

33. If you are instructed to cut glass tubing, fire-polish the ends immediately to remove sharp edges.

34. Never use broken or chipped glassware. If glassware breaks, notify your teacher and dispose of the glassware in the proper trash container.

35. Never eat or drink from laboratory glassware. Thoroughly clean glassware before putting it away.

Using Sharp Instruments

36. Handle scalpels or razor blades with extreme care. Never cut material toward you; cut away from you.

37. Immediately notify your teacher if you cut your skin when working in the laboratory.

Animal Safety

38. No experiments that will cause pain, discomfort, or harm to mammals, birds, reptiles, fishes, and amphibians should be done in the classroom or at home.

39. Animals should be handled only if necessary. If an animal is excited or frightened, pregnant, feeding, or with its young, special handling is required.

40. Your teacher will instruct you as to how to handle each animal species that may be brought into the classroom.

41. Clean your hands thoroughly after handling animals or the cage containing animals.

End-of-Experiment Rules

42. After an experiment has been completed, clean up your work area and return all equipment to its proper place.

43. Wash your hands after every experiment.

44. Turn off all burners before leaving the laboratory. Check that the gas line leading to the burner is off as well.

Glossary

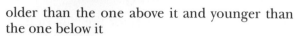

adaptation: change that increases an organism's chances of survival

adaptive radiation: process by which a species evolves into several species, each of which fills a different niche

cast: fossil in which the space left behind in a rock by a dissolved organism has filled, showing the same shape of the organism

Cro-Magnon (kroh-MAG-nuhn): early human that lived 40,000 years ago; *Homo sapiens sapiens*

evolve: to change over time

evolution: change in species over time

extrusion: igneous rock formation that forms on the Earth's surface

fault: break or crack along which rock moves

fossil: remains or evidence of a living thing

half-life: amount of time it takes for one half of the atoms of a sample of a radioactive element to decay

homologous (hoh-MAH-luh-guhs) **structure:** structure that evolves from similar body parts

imprint: fossil formed when a thin object leaves an impression in soft mud, which hardens

index fossil: fossil of an organism that existed on Earth for only a short period of time and that can be used by scientists to determine the relative age of a rock

intrusion: irregular formation of intrusive rock formed by magma beneath the Earth's crust

law of superposition: law that states that in undisturbed sedimentary rocks each layer is older than the one above it and younger than the one below it

mold: fossil formed in a rock by a dissolved organism that leaves an empty space, showing its outward shape

molecular clock: scale used to estimate the rate of change in proteins over time

natural selection: survival and reproduction of those organisms best adapted to their surroundings

Neanderthal: early human that lived 150,000 years ago to about 35,000 years ago; *Homo neanderthalensis* (nee-AN-der-thawl-ehn-sihs)

niche: combination of an organism's needs and its habitat

petrification: process by which once-living material is replaced by minerals, turning it into stone

primate: member of a group of animals that includes humans, monkeys, and about 200 other species of living things

punctuated equilibrium: periods in Earth's history in which many adaptive radiations occur in a relatively short period of time

sediment: small pieces of rock, shell, and other material that are broken down over time

trace fossil: mark or evidence of the activities of an organism

unconformity: eroded rock surface, pushed up from deeper within the Earth, that is much older than the new rock layers above it

Index

Credits